Songs Of The Cowboy

Compiled by Ron Middlebrook   **Foreward by** Tom Chambers

Featuring songs by:

Riders In The Sky, Marty Robbins, Michael Martin Murphey,
Tom Chambers, Gary McMahan, Eddie Dean, Joel Reese,
Robert Wagoner, Poetry by Reine River

Wyoming State Archives, Museums and Historical Department

Special Thanks to Gary Zimmerman

Cover Art-**Eddie Young**
Music Notation-**Steve Barden**
Music Transcribing-**George Ports**
Layout & Production-**Ron Middlebrook**

ISBN 0-931759-46-3
SAN 683-8022

Lucky 4

CONTENTS

FOREWORD

Throughout history, folk music has served the roll as sentinel for cultures and nations around the world. There is no better example of history being protrayed through the verses of song than the melodies and lyrics that have evolved in the American West. The romance attached to the cowboy and his free roaming life style has been created largely though the musical accounts that have been composed in tribute to this American hero.

The early verses set to the familiar European melodies were the humble origins of a musical documentation which has continued to trace the growth and development of the western frontier for more than 130 years. Through this long and colorful development, there have been those dedicated individuals who have documented this musical history and preserved it for future generations. Names such as Thorpe, Lomax, Fife, Tinsley, Griffis and Cannon will be remembered as historians as well as authors, because their volumes have accurately captured the evolution of the music which reflects the landscape, people and myths of the West. In his book "Song of the Cowboy", Ron Middlebrook has once again updated the pages of history. He has combined the classic cowboy songs with the romantic silver screen compositions and has then recognized the continued growth of Western music by including some of the most current works of today's cowboy songwriters. This book will certainly take a prominent place in the collections of those who appreciate our Western musical heritage.

Tom Chambers, Pres.
Western Music Association, Inc.

**WESTERN
MUSIC
ASSOCIATION**

Help celebrate the Music of the American West and become a member of the Western Music Association and join with others who love and treasure western music. The Western Music Association was formed to get western music out from behind the chutes and back into the arena where it belongs. With annual music festivals by the top performers today, workshops and clinics on all aspects of western music.
For more information contact:
**Western Music Association, Inc.
P.O. Box 64852
Tucson, AZ 85740
(602) 577-8055**

INTRODUCTION

The first cowboys were Texans who, for reasons we do not yet understand, found most of their ballad models in northern states. The cattle business had its beginnings in the southern part of Texas that lies along the Gulf Coast, an ideal breeding ground for wild cattle which the patriotic, quick-shooting Anglos from Tennessee preempted from the Mexican ranchers. From the Mexican *vaquero* they acquired their tools and their costume-the *sombrero,* the chaps (*chaparajos*), the *reata,* the Mexican high-cantle saddle, etc. - and from him they learned the art of handling cattle, which included calling to the cattle and singing to them.

Before the Civil War, Texas cattle were slaughtered for their hides and the hides shipped out on coastal barques to the East; but the longhorns had multiplied so rapidly in south Texas during the Civil War, that the ranchers began looking for ways to move their portable wealth north to the middle-western railheads. The first trail herds tried a direct route through the Ozarks to St Louis, but they were bushwacked by outlaws, the cowboys murdered, and the cattle driven into the hills. Then an enterprising promoter named Colonel Dodge persuaded the Missouri Pacific R. R. to run a spur out into the Kansas plains, and, when this news filtered down into South Texas, big trail heads of longhorns were started north to meet the railroad.

The Texas trail bosses pushed their heads north across the plains to Kansas. The Old Chisholm Trail they blazed soon ran all the way to Montana, and the great plains country - formerly the absolute domain of the mounted Plains Indians - quickly filled up with ranches. The trail period lasted no more than twenty years, between 1870 and 1890, but this was sufficient time for the untrammelled genius of the westerners to improvise a culture suitable to themselves.

America's love affair with the cowboy dates back at least to the days when Buffalo Bill Cody began assembling ropers and riders for his Wild West Shows. The notion of the West as the last frontier, where "men are men"-self-reliant, decisive, free individuals-values are clear-cut and justice is swift, persists to this day. In our era of increasing urbanization and regimentation, it's small wonder that we revere the life and times we associate with the westward expansion and settlement of our nation.

Part of this love for simpler, better days finds expression in the continued popularity of Western music and the great themes and exciting images that keep it alive and vital. The cowboys and their successors sang of the beauty of nature, the virtue of women, the comradeship of men. And they told stories of how the railroads moved West, of the great cattle drives, of what a cowboy said as he lay dying, of the light in the eyes of a gay senorita.

This collection is a saddlebag full of the old and the new, the authentic and the romantic, the factual and the fictional songs that helped build the legend of the Old West. All of them are known and loved, and many of them are often heard today.

The earliest are true folk songs, sung by the early pioneers of country music, authentic cowboys like Carl T. Sprague and Jules Verne Allen who went from the West to the recording studios of New Your.

All of the songs are classics-true at least in spirit to the pioneers who , with six-gun or telegraph key or guitar, help to win and populate the Western states - to their pathos, their humor, their hijinks and, above all, their abiding romantic love for the prairies west of the Mississippi.

And they're sung and played by the great Western stars who in our youth helped form our notions of what the West was like and how we should think about good and evil. Gene Autry, Roy Rogers, Tex Ritter, The Sons of the Pioneers-these were the people who set the tumbleweeds tumbling in our hearts. So, settle back and be transported to the Old West, Get into the saddle and slip into the easy rhythm of the cattle drive, polish up your six-shooter and live again the exciting days of the frontier, spread your gear around the campfire and, along with your saddle pals, sing these great songs of the cowboy.

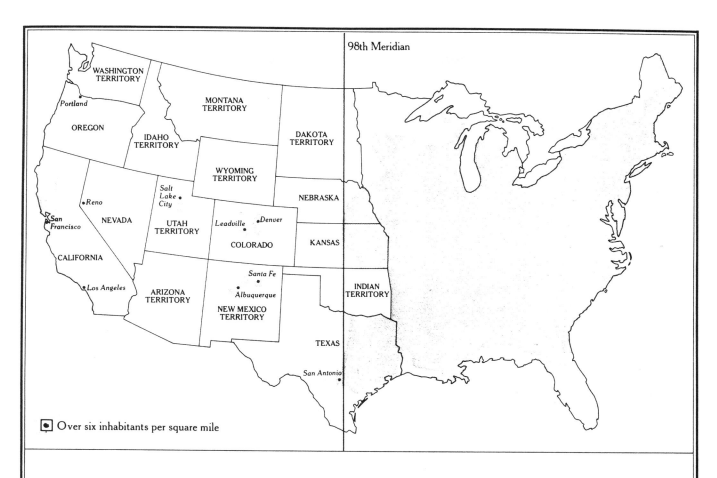

Over six inhabitants per square mile

The view from the fastidious East

In 1876, the centennial of the Declaration of Independence, the U.S. was still divided into two parts, one settled, one wild. The boundary between them was the 98th meridian, a line where diminishing annual rainfall caused Eastern forests to stop and grasslands to begin. To the east 31 states were settled by 42 million people. To the west of the meridian lay all or parts of seven states and nine territories, populated by a mere two million souls. The few towns of any size were scattered across an enormous territory whose uncivilized land and peoples had long been scorned by even the most farsighted Easterners.

It is to be feared that a great part of [the West] will form a lawless interval between the abodes of civilized men. . . . Here may spring up new and mongrel races, like new formations in geology, the amalgamation of the "debris" and "abrasions" of former races.

Washington Irving, 1836

What do we want with this vast, worthless area? This region of savages and wild beasts, of deserts, shifting sands and whirlwinds of dust, of cactus and prairie dogs? . . . I will never vote one cent from the public treasury [for postal service] to place

the Pacific Coast one inch nearer to Boston than it now is.

Daniel Webster, 1838

We seem to have reached the acme of barrenness and desolation.

Horace Greeley, 1859

Sometimes we have the seasons [in Nevada] in their regular order, and then again we have winter all the summer and summer all winter. . . . It is mighty regular about not raining, though. . . . But as a general thing . . . the climate is good, what there is of it.

Mark Twain, circa 1865

By 1860 Texas herds had grown to some 3.5 million head, then came a hiatus that was to last for five years: while their cattle, untended and undriven, continued to multiply on the open range, ranchers and cowboys went off to fight in the Civel War.

Right atfer the Civil War, most of the longhorns were wandering, lost in the vastness of the Texas brush country. Charles Goodnight later recalled, "Certain scattered men over the country could not resist the temptation and went to branding those catle for themselves." He estimated that in Texas there were two or three mavericks-unbranded calves-for every branded one. The word maverick itself carried a warning. It came from Sam Maverick, a cattleman on the San Antonio River who neglected his branding and discovered, after only a year of ranching on this rich, well-watered ground, that he had been forced out of business by avaricious neighbors and outright rustlers who had made off with his unmarked stock.

5

Lonely Yukon Stars

Words and Music by Douglas B. Green

[Yodel, repeat last four lines]

Lonely Yukon stars gleaming bright in the sky,
Scattered careless and loving by an artist on high.
To their silent song the sighing wind adds its part,
A song that can only be heard by the heart.

Northern lights that hang, pale curtains of fire,
Lead me to the one waiting warm by the fire.
Lightly goes the moon on its melancholy way,
Guiding me onward as night becomes day.

That's How The Yodel Was Born

(The true and painful story where the cowboy learned to yodel)

Words and Music by Douglas B. Green

Fancy yodel and out

When you hear a cowboy yodeling a song of open range,
Your heart leaps up to hear his stirring tale.
But did you every wonder at the end of his refrain,
Why his voice breaks in a mournfull wail?
The story as its told to me was handed down in history
Of a singing cowboy bold enough to try,

To ride the meanest old cayuse, it bucked him off
Right at the chute and left him spinning way up in the sky.
The broncho jumped up and the cowboy came down.
They met at the old saddle horn.
It made a deep impression, you could say it changed his life.
And that's how the yodel was born.

Bobby Beeman

Don Putnam

Riders In The Sky

For a catolog of all the Riders In The Sky merchandise send to
Too Slim's Mercantile - P.O. Box 277, White's Creek, TN 37189

THE EVOLUTION OF THE COWBOY BOOT

Early cowhands wore flat-heeled, round-toed boots they brought home from the Civil War. In the 1860s the true cowboy boot appeared featuring a reinforced arch and higher heel. Later boots took on semi-functional frills, such as a more pointed toe and floppy grips called mule ears to make them easier to pull on. The fanciest boots, made after the mid-1880s, were of soft leather with decorative stitching, which some cowboys claimed gave a snugger fit.

Early   Cowboy heel   Mule ear   Fancy

SPURS FOR RANGE WORK AND DISPLAY

Highly practical, spurs were also a vital part of the cowboy's image, and he rarely took them off. The spur's heel band fit over the back of the boot, while the spur strap fastened across the instep. The heel chain not only kept the spur from riding up but, along with the jinglebobs, produced a sound that was music to any strutting cowboy's ears. Most Americans shunned Mexican spurs, with their spiky rowels, and used models like the OK, with rowels filed down to avoid scouring the pony's flanks. The plainest type was a work spur, with a gentle, star-shaped rowel. However, many cowboys also owned a pair of fancy silver spurs like those shown at lower right.

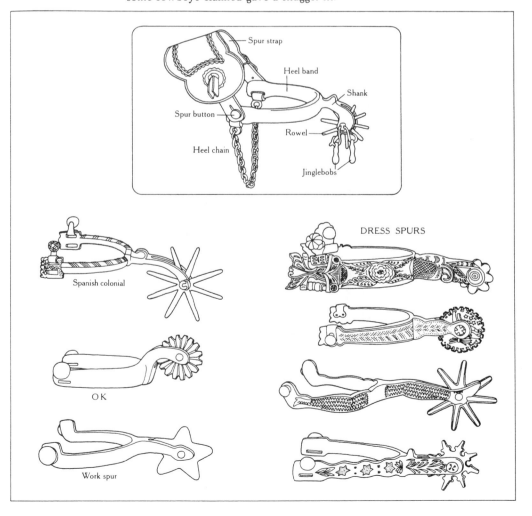

Spur strap

Heel band

Shank

Spur button

Rowel

Heel chain

Jinglebobs

Spanish colonial

DRESS SPURS

OK

Work spur

Canyons Of My Mind

Lyrics and Music by
Tom Chambers

(Fiddle break)

Clos- est thing to heav- en I have ev - er seen is that rug - ged un - spoiled coun - try where my mind is free to dream Cour - age has the room to grow where na - ture has con - trol and con - tent - ment is the state of mind that can't be bought or sold

CHORUS I love those snow-capped moun-tains and the des - erts far be - low from the blue Can - a - di - an Rock - ies to the hills of Mex - i - co It's the place where na - ture comes to rest this land that I call mine I'm rid - in' through the sun - sets of the can - yons in my mind Yes I'm rid - in' through the sun - sets of the can - yons of my mind

Silloettes of granite peaks 'cross a painted sky,
Echos songs of hearty pioneers and tales of days gone by.
Oh the trails so seldom traveled are the ones that I love best
As I gaze across the skyline of this land they call the west.

Chorus
I love those snowcapped mountains and the deserts far below,
From the blue Canadian Rockies to the hills of Mexico.
It's the place where nature comes t rest this land that I call mine,
I'm ridin' through the sunsets of the canyons of my mind.

Closest thing to heaven I have ever seen
Is that rugged unspoiled country where my mind is free to dream.
Courage has the room to grow where nature has control
And contentment is the state of mind that can't be bought or sold.

Chorus
Yes I'm ridin' through the sunsets of the canyons of my mind.

The Chambers

Cassette Tape of Tom Chambers
Tom & Becki Chambers, with the Sons of the Western Plains
P.O. Box 65052
Tucson, AZ 85740

Joyce Woodson

Circle B Cowboys

13

Wild Mustang

Words and Music by Robert Wagoner

He's des - ert bred he's un - der - fed and tough as a pin - ion tree _____ no

cow - boy pals or home cor - rals just wild and run - nin' free _____ no

things of beau - ty most would say but beau - ty's hid - den there _____ It's

in the blood of a rang - y stud and the heart of a mus - tang mare _____ A

rock- y rim is home to him he roams the end - less sand _____ where

coy - otes wail on the des - ert trail of his lone - ly wand - 'rin' band _____

Sto - ries told by cow - boys bold and songs of him they sang _____ tell

plain - tive - ly how great must be the heart of the wild mus - tang.

He's desert bred, he's underfed and tough as a Pinion tree
No cowboy pals or home corrals just wild and runnin' free
No thing of beauty most would say but beauty's hidden there
It's in the blood of a rangy stud and the heart of a mustang mare.

A rocky rim is home to him, he roams the endless sand
Where coyotes wail on the desert trail of his loney wandrn' band.
Stories told by cowboy's bold and songs of him they sang
Tell plaintively how great must be the heart of the wild mustang.

He'll come in sight some starry night across a sandy dune
Or standin' high against the sky beneath a desert moon.
His coat is rough his nature tough his disposition mild
This mustang steed was born to heed the call of the western wild.

His color might be kinda red, buckskin, white or dun
Grulla, gray, black or bay or the color of the sun.
Stories told by cowboy's bold and songs of him they sang
Tell plaintively how great must be the heart of the wild mustang.

Robert Wagoner

M arty Robbins was one of the greatest story tellers, it came easy, for his grandfather, "Texas" Bob Heckle was his first hero. "He was a great old character, and he could tell the best stories and biggest lies of any man I ever knew," Marty told Country Music magazine. "He was a real medicine man. Had his own show. They ran him out of Texas for stealing horses. Oh, he told me he was a Texas Ranger; that was just one of his big lies." Marty and his grandfather made a deal: Texas Bob would tell him a tale of the Old West, and Marty would sing his grandfather a song. "I did that from the time I was three or four until he died when I was six.

"I would have liked to have lived in the Old West," he summed up for Music City News. "I would like to have been born in 1820, and if I'd been born back then, I would definitely have been a gunfighter. I probably would not have been an outlaw. I believe I would have been a lawman."

The next 7 songs are from Marty's gunfighter albums. Two are written by him "The Red Hills Of Utah" and "The Masters Call."

Abilene Rose

All you young cow-boys come gath-er a-round. I'll tell you a stor-y of Ab-i-lene town, of two young lov-ers as true lov-ers know the girl in the stor-y is Ab-i-lene Rose. Rose Rose Ab-i-lene Rose, your mem-'ry still lives in my heart. _____ Rose _____ Ab-i-lene Rose, we prom-ised we nev-er would part.

1. All you young cowboys come gather around.
   I'll tell you a story of Abilene town.
   Of two young lovers as true lovers know.
   The girl in the story is Abilene Rose.
   Chorus
   Rose, Rose, Abilene Rose,
   Your mem'ry still lives in my heart.
   Rose, Abilene Rose,
   We Promised we never would part.

2. Rose was so pretty in her gingham gown.
   She was the fairest in Abilene town.
   Her eyes were as bright as the stars up above.
   Everyone knew when she chose me to love.
   Chorus

3. We courted each other out under the moon.
   We planned to be married the first day of June.
   Then I started drinking and gambling you see.
   I broke her young heart, and then she left me.
   Chorus

4. I got into trouble and had to leave town.
   Rose got married and then settled down.
   She was as happy as happy could be.
   With her young cowboy and their family.
   Chorus:

5. This is the story I promised to tell.
   All you young cowboys remember it well.
   If you find true love don't tear it apart.
   Marry that true love don't break her young heart.
   Rose, Rose, Abilene Rose,
   Your mem'ry still lives in my heart.
   Rose, Abilene Rose,
   Forever we must live apart.

Doggone Cowboy

Never mind that the harsh realities of trail life could degrade a man to the point of forcing him to lick horse sweat from a saddle when the chuck wagon ran out of salt. And never mind, either, that in return for three to four months of dust, thirst, blisters, cold and danger the cowboy received a paltry $100 in hard wages-barely the price of a new hat and a fancy pair of boots. Is the cowboy in this song one spur short at a rodeo or what? He really loves his work!

Words and Music by
Joe Babcock

1. I'm into the rovin' wind
   That brings the northern in.
   Along that dusty trail
   I'll take my stand
   The steers are big and bold
   And the nights are often cold,
   But I'll get by as long as I can...

Chorus
   Throw that rope and brand that calf
   Dream of a girl in a photograph.
   I got no home, I got no wife,
   But I'll be a doggone cowboy all of my life.

2. I'm up at the crack of dawn,
   And I throw the bacon on.
   Seems somehow my work is never through.
   When I get done at night
   All the stars are big and bright.
   But then it's all sort of what you're used to when you...
   Chorus

3. The hot dry wind may blow,
   And you'll see me in the rain and snow,
   With just an ol' camp fire to keep me warm,
   I'll move the herd along
   And I'll greet them with a song.
   So I guess I was born to...
   Chorus

Red Hills Of Utah

Words and Music by
Marty Robbins

1. How green are the valleys
   How tall are the trees
   How cool are the rivers
   How soft is the breeze

   If it's just like my dreams
   Then I must go and see
   For the Red Hills of Utah
   Are callin' me.

   So long I have waited
   Since I was a child,
   Merely the thought keeps
   My heart running wild.
   I've waited so long
   Now its hard to believe
   The Red Hills of Utah
   At last I will see.

2. How pretty are flowers
   That bloom in the spring
   How sweet are the songs
   The mockin' bird sing.

   If it's just like my dreams
   Then I must go and see
   For the Red Hills of Utah
   Are callin' me.

The Fastest Gun Around

There's always someone wanting to be the badest, and meanest one around, and if Joey could gun down
Billy the kid, he would be those plus the fastest gun. But Joey was no match for Bill's lightin' draw. This
new song gives Billy a conscience, those that knew him said he had none.

Words and Music by
Jean Pruett and Jim Glaser

notch-es on his gun, and he wished that he could give him these he carved up- on his own Joe-y's hand went to his side; he was sure that he had won, but be-fore he ev-en fired he saw the smoke of Bill-y's gun, an' he felt the bull-et hit him hard an' be-fore his eyes he saw his wast-ed life passed quick-ly end-ing with his fat-al draw.

(2) round.

In the days of William Bonney,	Billy knew that Joey wanted
Better known as Bill the kid,	Notches on his gun,
A young cowboy named Joey,	And he wished that he could give him those
Still was bound to make his bid.	He carved upon his own.
Well, he heard one day that Bill the kid	Joey's hand went to his side,
Had just rode into town.	He was sure that he had won,
And if he could take him he would be	But before he even fired,
The Fastest Gun Around.	He saw the smoke of Billy's gun.
He was just a kid of seventeen,	And he felt the bullet hit him hard,
But he had a lighten' hand.	Before his eyes he saw,
And he said it's time I showed	His wasted life passed quickly ending
The world that I'd become a man.	With his fatal draw.
Everyone thinks Billy is	Billy breathed more easily
The Fastest Gun Around,	And he put away his gun,
But they will know I'm faster	And he tried to ease his conscience
When they see me shoot him down.	For the wrong that he had done.
They finally came together down on	And he saddled up his horse
Main Street just in time,	And he headed westward out of town
The people were all gathered wonderin'	And he wondered just how long he'd be
Who'd be left alive.	The Fastest Gun Around.

The Master's Call

A cowboy converted in the face of death. One of Marty's lesser known, but one of his best written songs.

Words and Music by
Marty Robbins

When I was but a young man I was wild and full of fire, a

youth with-in my teens but full of chal-lenge and de-sire I

run-a-way from home and left my moth-er and my dad. I

know it grieved them so to think their on-ly boy was bad. One

night we wrest-led cat-tle, a thous-and head or so start-ed then out on the trail at

leads to Mex-i-co. When a North-ern start-ed blow-in' and light-nin' flashed a-bout, I

thought some-one was call-in' me I thought I heard a shout

At that mo-ment light-ning struck not twen-ty yards from me and left there was a gi-ant cross where

once there was a tree and this time I knew I heard a voice, a voice so sweet and strange, a

voice that came from ev-ery-where, a voice that called my name.

When I was but a young man I was wild and full of fire,
A youth within my teens but full of challenge and desire.
I runaway from home and left my mother and my dad,
I know it grieved them so to think their only boy was bad.

I fell in with an outlaw band, their names were known quite well.
How many times we robbed and plundered I could never tell.
This kind of sinful living leads only to a fall,
I learned that much and more that night I heard my master's call.

One night we wrestled cattle, a thousand head or so
Started then out on the trail that leads to Mexico.
When a Northern started blowin' and lightnin' flashed about,
I thought someone was callin' me I thought I heard a shout.

At that moment lightning struck not twenty yards from me,
And left there was a giant cross where once there was a tree.
And this time I knew I heard a voice, a voice so sweet and strange,
A voice that came from everywhere, a voice that called my name.

So frightened I was thinking of sinful deeds I'd done,
I failed to see the thousand head of cattle start to run.
The cattle they stampeded, were runnin' all around,
My pony ran but stumbled and it threw me to the ground.

I felt the end was nearing that death would be the price.
When a mighty bolt of lighting showed the face of Jesus Christ.
And I cried 'oh lord forgive me, don't let it happen now.
I want to live for you alone, oh God these words I vow.'

My wicked life unfolded, I thought of wasted years.
When another bolt of lighting killed a hundred head of steers,
And the others rushed on by me, and I was left to live.
The Master had a reason life was his to take or give.

A miracle performed that night I wasn't meant to die,
The dead ones formed a barracade nearly six or seven high.
And right behind it there was I, afraid but safe and sound.
I cried in vain for mercy nealing there upon the ground.

A pardon I was granted, my sinfull soul set free,
No more to fear the angry waves upon life's stormy sea.
Forgiven by the love of God, a love that will remain,
I gave my life and soul the night the savior called my name.

The Strawberry Roan

Though it has the flair of a traditional cowboy song, this was written as a long narrative poem in 1915 by famed rodeo rider Curley Fletcher. Fletcher ran short of money and offered to sell the lyric to popular songwriter Nat Vincent for $200. Instead, Vincent gave him a full share of royalties-plus the cash-and turned it into a classic ballad. Ken Maynard and Gene Autry sang it and used it as the title song for their individual films. A strawberry roan is a horse with a basic sorrel color and a uniform mixture of white hairs over the entire body.

I was hang-ing 'round town not earn-ing a dime, Be-ing out of a

job, just a-spend-ing my time. When a stran-ger steps up and he

says, 'I sup-pose That you're a bronc rid-er by the looks of your clothes.'

I says, 'Guess you're right, and a good one I claim. Do you hap-pen to

have an-y bad ones to tame?' He says, 'I've got one that's a

good one to buck At throw-ing good rid-ers, he's had lots of luck.'

1. I was hanging 'round town not earning a dime,
   Being out of a job, just a-spending my time.
   When a stranger steps up and he says, 'I suppose
   That you're a bronc rider by the looks of your clothes.'
   I says, 'Guess you're right, and a good one I claim.
   Do you happen to have any bad ones to tame?'
   He says, 'I've got one, that's a good one to buck.
   At throwing good riders, he's had lots of luck.'

2. I gits all excited and asks what he pays
   To ride that old horse for a couple of days.
   He offers me ten, and I says, 'I'm your man,
   'Cause the horse hasn't lived that I couldn't fan.'
   He says, 'Git your saddle, and I'll give you a chance.'
   So we climb in the buckboard and ride to the ranch.
   Early next morning right after chuck
   I go down to see if this outlaw can buck.

24

3. There in the corral just a-standing alone
   Is a scrawny old pony - a strawberry roan.
   He has little pig eyes and a big Roman nose,
   Long spavined legs that turn in at the toes,
   Little pin ears that are split at the tip,
   And a 44 brand there upon his left hip.
   I put on my spurs and I coil up my twine,
   And say to the stranger, 'That ten-spot is mine.'

4. Then I put on the blinds and it sure is a fight.
   My saddle comes next, and I screw it down tight.
   Then I pile on his back and well I know then,
   If I ride this old pony, I'll sure earn my ten.
   For he bows his old neck and he leaps from the ground
   Ten circles he makes before he comes down.
   He's the worse bucking bronc I've seen on the range,
   He can turn on a nickel and give you some change.

5. He goes up again and he turns round and round.
   As if he's quit living down there on the ground.
   He turns his old belly right up to the sun;
   He sure is a sunfishing son-of-a-gun.
   He goes up in the East and comes down in the West.
   To stay in the saddle, I'm doin' my best.
   I lose both my stirrups and also my hat,
   And start pullin' leather as blind as a bat.

6. He goes up once more, and he goes way up high,
   And leaves me a-settin' up there in the sky.
   I turn over twice and I come down to earth,
   And I start into cussin' the day of his birth.
   I've rode lots of ponies out here on the range,
   And there's been one or two that I shore couldn't tame.
   But I'll bet all my money there's no man alive
   Can ride that old horse when he makes his high dive.

Gene Autry

25

Utah Carroll

The legend of a cowboy who died in turning the running herd, to save a ranchman's little daughter. The cowboy way: reverence for perfect womanhood even to the point of giving one's life to preserve it. A very long song and often shorten in performance. This song was a favorite of Ken Maynard, the first singing cowboy movie star.

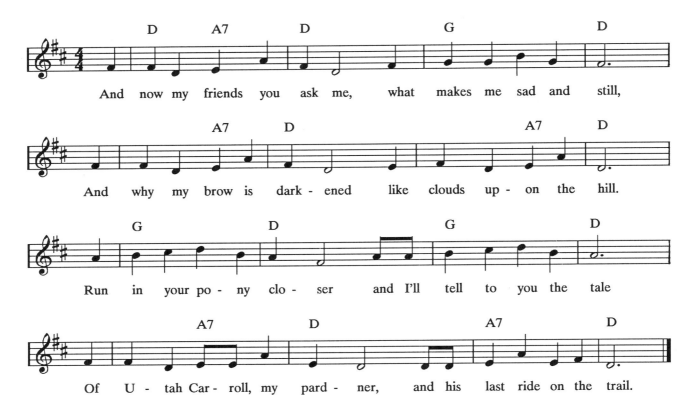

1. And now my friends you ask me, what makes me sad and still,
   And why my brow is darkened like clouds upon the hill.
   Run in your pony closer and I'll tell to you the tale
   Of Utah Carrol, my pardner, and his last ride on the trail.

2. In the cactus and the thistle of Mexico's fair land,
   Where cattle roam in thousands in many a herd and brand.
   There's a grave without a headstone, with neither date nor name,
   Where my pardner sleeps in silence in the land from which I came.

3. We roamed the range together, we rode it side by side.
   I loved him like a brother and I wept when Utah died.
   Side by side we rode the roundups, we roped and burned the brand,
   Through storm and dreary darkness, we joined the night herd stand.

4. While rounding up one morning, our work was nearly done,
   When off the cattle started on a mad and fearful run.
   The boss's little daughter, who was riding on that side,
   Rushed in to turn the cattle, and there my pardner died.

5. She saw the cattle charging and turned her pony round.
   Her bright red blanket loosened and dragged upon the ground.
   She leaned and lost her balance, fell in front of that wild tide.
   'Lie still Lenore, I'm coming,' were the words that Utah cried.

6. Some fifty yards behind her, Utah came riding fast.
   But little did he know that this ride would be his last.
   His pony reached the maiden with a firm and steady bound,
   And he swung out from his saddle to lift her off the ground.

7. But the strain upon the saddle had not been felt before,
   The hind cinch snapped beneath him and he fell beside Lenore.
   Utah picked up the blanket and waved it o'er his head;
   He raced across the prairie. 'Lie still, Lenore,' he said.

8. My pardner turned the stampede and saved his little frend,
   But the maddened cattle rushed him, and he turned to meet his end.
   His six-gun flashed like lightning; it sounded lou and clear.
   As the cattle charged upon him, he dropped the leading steer.

9. Then on his funeral morning, I heard the preacher say,
   'I hope we'll all meet Utah in the roundup far away.'
   Then he wrapped him in a blanket, sent by his little friend.
   It was that same red blanket that brought him to his end.

Chinks

Ken Maynard

Tall In The Saddle

Words and Music by
Joel Reese

1. Before there were fences it was all open range
   The sky went forever on the Oklahoma plains.
   And there were cattle drives northward on the Old Chisolm Trail,
   He was tougher than leather 'cause his work was pure hell.

2. Well he rode endless miles thru the wind and the rain,
   To gather stray calves and wild horses to tame.
   You know his work was his life until his last days,
   He was hell-bent for leather but there was Heaven in his ways. *Chorus*

Chorus
   He stood tall in the saddle and strong against the wind,
   He respected a lady and gave to no end.
   He'd feed a stranger or return a stray cow,
   We could sure use a cowboy right now.

28

Joel Reese

Cassette tape of Joel Reese
'Odds & Ends'
28701 Merjanian Rd.
Menifee, CA 92355

On a Western saddle each part evolved to meet a specific cowboy need, from the horn for roping to the broad stirrups in which the cowboy stood when he was riding down steep slopes or trotting along the trail.

The number of cows trailed out of Texas rose dramatically for the first five years of the great drives, then dropped due to a market glut in 1871 and a depression two years later.

Box score for the big years	
1867.	35,000
1868.	75,000
1869.	350,000
1870.	300,000
1871.	600,000
1872.	350,000
1873.	405,000
1874.	166,000
1875.	151,618
1876.	321,998
1877.	201,159
1878.	265,646
1879.	257,927
1880.	394,784
1881.	250,000

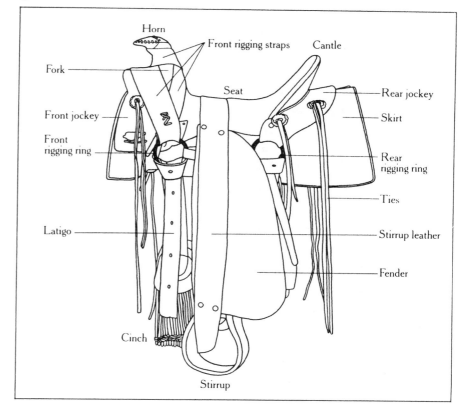

Michael Martin Murphey

Michael Martin Murphey
"Cowboy Songs"
Warner Bros.Records, Inc.

Red River Valley

Originally a Canadian love song, with the Red River of the North as its setting, it became a cowboy song about the Red River of the Texas-Oklahoma cattle country and it gained widespread appeal to finally become one of the favorite folk songs of America.

1. From this valley they say you are going,
   I will miss your bright eyes and sweet smile.
   For they say you are taking the sunsine.
   That has brightened our pathway awhile.

   Chorus
   Come and sit by my side if you love me.
   Do not hasten to bid me adieu.
   But remember the Red River Valley
   And the cowboy that loves you so true.

2. From this valley they say you are going,
   I will miss your sweet face and your smile.
   Just because you are weary and tired,
   You are changing your range for awhile.

   Chorus

3. I've been waiting a long time my darling
   For the sweet words you never would say.
   Now at last all my fond hopes have vanished,
   For they say you are going away.

   Chorus

4. O there never could be such a longing
   In the heart of a poor cowboy's breast.
   That now dwells in the heart you are breaking,
   As I wait in my home in the West.
   Chorus

5. Do you think of the valley you're leaving?
   O how lonely and drear it will be!
   Do you think of the kind heart you're breaking,
   And the pain you are causing to me?
   Chorus

6. As you go to your home by the ocean, May you never forget those sweet hours
   That we spent in the Red River Valley, And the love we exchanged mid the flowers.

   Chorus

31

Tying Knots In The Devil's Tail

One of the great cowboy brag songs.

By Gail I. Gardner

Way high up in the Sier - ry Peaks, Where the yel-low-jack pines grow tall, _____ Old

Bus - ter Jiggs and Sand - y Bob had a round-up camp last fall. _____

Way high up in the Sierry Peaks
Where the yellow-jack pines grow tall,
Old Buster Jiggs and Sandy Bob
Had a round-up camp last fall.

Well, they took along their running irons,
Maybe a dog or two,
And they 'lowed they'd brand every long-eared calf
That came within their view.

Now every little long-eared dogie
That didn't push up by day,
Got his long ears whittled and his old hide scorched
In a most artistic way.

One fine day, says Buster Jiggs,
As he throwed his seago down,
'I'm tired of cowpiography,
And I think I'm a-goin' into town.'

Well they saddled up their ponies and they hit a lope,
For it warn't no sight of a ride,
And them was the days that a good cow-punch
Could oil up his insides.

Well they started in at Kentucky Bar,
At the head of Whiskey Row,
And they wound her up at the Depot House
About forty drinks below.

Well they sets 'em up and they turns around,
And they started in the other way,
And to tell the God-forsaken truth
Them boys got drunk that day.

They was on their way, goin' back to camp,
A-packin' that awful load,
Who should they meet but the Devil himself
Come a-traipsin' down the road.

He says, 'You ornery cowboy skunks,
You better go hunt for your hole,
'Cause I've come up from Hell's rim rock
To gather in your souls.'

'The Devil be damned,' says Buster Jiggs,
'Us boys is a little bit tight,
But you don't go gatherin' no cowboys souls
Without one helluva fight.'

Now Buster Jiggs could ride like hell,
Throw a lasso, too,
So he threw it over the Devil's horns
And he took his dallies true.

Now Sandy Bob was a reata man,
With his gut-line coiled up neat,
But he shook her out and he builds a loop
And he roped the Devil's hind feet.

Well they stretches him out and they tails him down,
While the runnin'-irons were gettin' hot,
And they cropped and swallow-forked his ears
And they branded him up a lot.

Well they trimmed his horns way down to his head,
Tied ten knots in his tail for a joke,
And then they went off and left him there
Tied up to a little pin oak.

Now when you're way high up in the Sierry Peaks,
And you hear one hell of a wail,
Well you'll know it's just the Devil himself
Yellin' about them knots in his tail.

When The Work's All Done This Fall

A song about the dying wishes of a cowboy trampled in a stampede. The fear of a stampede was always on the minds of the cowboy on the trail. It took only one cow to start the mad dash and the others would join instantly. Stampedes were more common at night during thunderstorms.

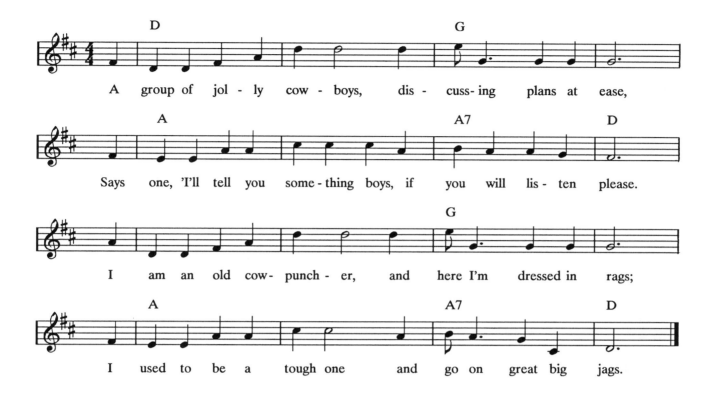

1. A group of jolly cowboys, discussing plans at ease,
   Says one, 'I'll tell you something boys, if you will listen please.
   I am an old cowpuncher, and here I'm dressed in rags;
   I used to be a tough one and go on great big jags.'

2. 'But I have got a home boys, and a good one you all know,
   Although I haven't seen it since long, long ago.
   I'm going back to Dixie once more to see them all;
   I'm going to see my mother when the work's all done this fall.'

3. 'When I left my home boys, my mother for me cried,
   She begged me not to go boys, for me she would have died.
   My mother's heart is breaking, breaking for me that's all,
   And with God's help I'll see her when the work's all done this fall.'

4. That very night this cowboy went out to stand his guard;
   The night was dark and cloudy and storming very hard.
   The cattle, they got frightened, and rushed in wild stampede,
   The cowboy tried to head them, while riding at full speed.

5. While riding in the darkness, so loudly did he shout,
   Trying his best to head them and turn the herd about.
   His saddle horse did stumble and on him it did fall,
   Now he won't see his mother when the work's all done this fall.

6. His body was so mangled, the boys all thought him dead.
   They picked him up so gently and laid him on a bed;
   He opened wide his blue eyes, and looking all around,
   He motioned to his comrades to sit near on the ground.

7. 'Boys, send mother my wages, the wages I have earned,
   For I am so afraid boys, the last steer I have turned.
   I'm going to a new range, I hear my Master's call,
   And I'll not see my mother when the work's all done this fall.'

8. 'Fred, you take my saddle; George, you take my bed;
   Bill, you take my pistol after I am dead.
   Then please think of me kindly when you look upon them all,
   For I'll not see my mother when the work's all done this fall.'

9. Poor Charlie was buried at sunrise, no tombstone at his head,
   Nothing but a little board, and this is what it said:
   'Charlie died at daybreak. He died from a fall.
   And he'll not see his mother when the work's all done this fall.'

Wild Rippling Water

This song is about the seduction of a maiden by the enchantment of music. Having satiated the maiden's love for music by his expertise at "fiddling," the cowboy turns suddenly brutal in his talk about the wife back home in Arizona. In an equal number of songs the cowboy is left to pine while the maiden moves on to better game.

As I was out walking, a-rambling one day
I spied a fair couple a-coming my way.
One was a cowboy, a brave one was he,
The other a lady and a beauty was she,
The other a lady and a beauty was she.

Way, 'Where are you going, my pretty fair maid?'
'Just down by the river, just down by the shade,
Just down by the river, just down by the spring,
To see the wild water and hear the nightingale sing,
See the wild rippling water and hear the nightingale sing.'

They hadn't been gone but an hour or so
When he drew from his satchel a fiddle and bow.
He tuned up his fiddle all on a high string
And played a tune over and over again,
And played a tune over and over again.

'Now,' says the cowboy, 'I should have been gone.'
'No, no,' said the maid, 'just play one more song.
I'd rather hear the fiddle played on one string
Than to see the wild water and hear the nightingale sing,
See the wild rippling water and hear the nightingale sing.'

He tuned up his fiddle and rosined his bow
And played her a lecture, he played it all low.
He played her a lecture all on the high string.
'Hark, hark,' said the maid, 'hear the nightingale sing,
Hark, hark,' said the maid, 'hear the nightingale sing.'

She says, 'Dear cowboy, will you marry me?'
'No, no, pretty maid, that never can be.
I've a wife in Arizona, a lady is she,
One wife and one ranch are plenty for me.
One wife and one ranch are plenty for me.

'I'll go to Mexico and I'll stay there one year,
I'll drink a lot of wine, I'll drink a lot of beer.
If I ever come back it will be in the spring
To see the wild water and hear the nightingale sing,
See the wild rippling water and hear the nightingale sing.'

Come all you young ladies, take warning from me,
Never place your affections in a cowboy so free;
He'll go away and leave you as mine left me,
Leave you rocking the cradle, singing 'Bye, oh baby,'
Leave you rocking the cradle, singing 'Bye, oh baby.'

Leaders of the long drives

"Our leaders were a pair of prairie steers named Broad and Crump," recalled cowhand Alonzo Mitchell, in deference to a pair of canny longhorns that had walked like drill sergeants at the head of a drove going up the Chisholm Trail to Kansas. Such bovine leaders were common on a drive. Indeed in virtually every herd the first day out a few dominant steers marched instinctively to the lead and stayed there. The other cows followed — across gullies, through rivers. Trail hands freely conceded it was the lead steers' initiative as much as the cowhands' prodding that kept the animals moving.

At the railhead these longhorned Pied Pipers usually went the way of the other cows — straight into the loading pens headed for slaughter. A few, however, proved so valuable on the trail that they were spared to lead again. Best known was Charles Goodnight's Old Blue, which during eight seasons led some 10,000 head to Dodge City. En route he wore a bell around his neck the sound of which other cows soon learned to follow. At night Old Blue would wander freely into camp and mooch handouts from the doting cowboys. After his last drive he retired to a comfortable pasture, and when he finally died at age 20 his horns were mounted in the Goodnight ranch office.

Cowboys on a drive advance in formation as shown in this diagram. While the trail boss rode ahead to scout for water and pasture, the cowhands rotated among the other positions.

Eddie Dean and Roscoe Ates

Eddie Dean was born in Hopkins County, Texas, is the seventh son of the seventh son, and born in the seventh month.

After making a name for himself in Chicago where he worked for all three networks he arrived in California in 1937. Eddie started in pictures with HOP-ALONG CASSIDY, making nine pictures. He went on to make more than 60 of his own films, he sang, acted and played.

Eddie was the first Western Star to be in Cinecolor, where he was featured in "Song In Old Wyoming." Few knew it was his idea that low-budget Westerns in color would mean box-office profits.

Eddie made some of the first recording for the Decca label, and has recorded for most of all the majors labels. His first national hit was *"I Dreamed Of A Hillbilly Heaven"*, which he was co-writer. Other great songs by the pen of Eddie are: *"One Has My Name, The Other Has My Heart"*, *"Fools Gold"*, *"Walk Beside Me"*, *"Cry Of A Broken Heart"*. Eddie was very kind to let us include one of his more poplar song in this book *"Sunny San Juan"*.

36

Sunny San Juan

Words and Music by
Eddie Dean and Glema Strange

On the banks of the sun - ny San Juan _____ watch- in' the riv - er roll on _____ Won - der - ing if it will reach the sea Won - der - ing where my old pal can be. At the foot of this old west - ern hill _____ I'm watch- ing and wait - ing here still All that's left of my schemes, is to sit with my dreams, on the banks of the sun - ny San Juan. _____

1. On the Banks of the Sunny San Juan,
   Watchin' the river roll on.
   Wondering if it will reach the sea,
   Wondering where my old pal can be.
   At the foot of this old western hill.
   I'm watching and waiting here still,
   All that's left of my schemes,
   Is to sit with my dreams,
   On the banks of the Sunny San Juan.

2. Roll on dear old river roll on,
   Carry this message to her.
   Tell her I'm lonesome forlorn and blue.
   Tel her I'm sending my love by you,
   All the days seems so dreary and long,
   Nothing seems right since you're gone.
   But, some day I may see,
   You come drifting to me,
   On your waves dear old Sunny San Juan.

Gary McMahan

Albums by Gary McMahan
Colorado Blue and **Saddle "Em Up and Go!**
Horse Apple Records
710 Lodgepole Drive
Bellvue, CO 80512

The daily strategy of a typical spring roundup focused on a moving chuck wagon from which the men fanned out in the morning and they circled back with the cattle for sorting and branding each afternoon.

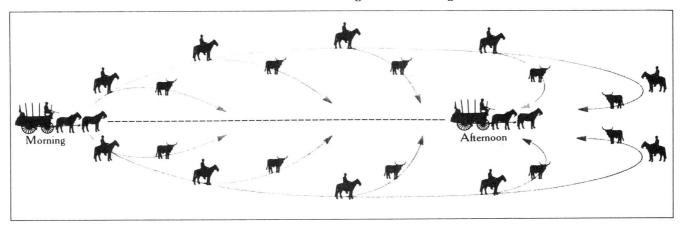

Real Live Buckaroo

Words & Music by
Gary McMahan

And whis-key tends to make me high, sad songs make me cry, pret-ty wo-men break my heart al-most ev-ery night; I run on beans and nic-o-tine, I'm a real live buck-a-roo; And my hearts not pure and my boots ain't clean and I ne-ver tell the truth; (And I smell like a litter of puppies and hardly ever tell te truth).

RECITATION 1

Now I ain't the type of cowboy that you see on T.V.;

I wasn't near as pretty as momma wanted me to be;

I grew up on the ranches, just a-cussin' all day long,

Breakin' in those broomtails and hummin' old dirty songs.

(CHORUS)

RECITATION 2

If there is anything under my hat, besides cooties and the cattle biz,

I just can't seem to remember what it is;

Yeah, my thinkin's kind of crude, but my lovin' gets plumb rank;

Them girlies don't understand me, snortin' in their flanks.

(CHORUS)

RECIATATION 3

And when I takes a nasty fall, I'll cuss it till I'm blue,

Then get right up and on again, just like you're s'posed to do;

Yeah I've been busting horses ever since I's a child

And I still can't tame wild horses, but I can make a tame horse wild.

Now, this song ain't about a Strawberry Roan, or a rampagin' herd of steers;

This is just the type of cowboy song, you pry don't want to hear;

This song ain't got a message, won't feel pretty in your ear;

This song is just one of them there -- well, this song is one of them there these heres.

(CHORUS)

The Old Double Diamond

Words & Music by
Gary McMahan

Moderately

win-ters and bust-ed her hor-ses; I took more than I thought I could stand; But the
bat-tle with the moun-tains and cat-tle _____ will bring out the best in a man;
I guess a sai-lor, he needs an o-cean, ____ and a mom-ma her ba-bies to hold.
And I need the hills of Wy-o-ming ____ in the land of the Buf - fa - lo;
Now she's sel-lin' out and I'm mov-in' on, but I'm leav-ing with more than I
came; 'Cause I got this sad - dle and it ain't for sale and I got this song to sing;
I've got a new range to find and new knots to tie, in a coun - try where
cow - boys are king; turned tails to the wind and the old Dou-ble Dia-mond
dis-ap - peared in - to the sage;

Oh, the old Double Diamond lay out east of Dubois,
In the land of the Buffalo;
And the auctioneer's gavel rapped and it rattled,
As I watched the old Double Diamond go.

Won't you listen to the wind,
Mother Nature's violin.

When I first hired on the old Double Diamond,
I's a damned poor excuse for a man.
I never learned how to aim,
Well, my spirit was tame,
I couldn't see all the cards in my hand.

And the wind whipped the granite above me,
And blew the tumbleweeds clean through my soul.

Well, I fought her winters and busted her horses,
I took more than I thought I could stand.
But the battle with the mountains and cattle
Will bring out the best in a man.

I guess a sailor, he needs an ocean,
And a momma her babies to hold.
And I need the hills of Wyoming
In the land of the Buffalo.

Now she's sellin' out and I'm movin' on,
But I'm leaving with more than I came.
'Cause I got this saddle and it ain't for sale
And I got this song to sing.

I've got a new range to find and new knots to tie,
In a country where cowboys are king.
Turned tails to the wind,
And the old Double Diamond disappeared into the sage.

41

The heraldry of the branding iron

Arizona cowpuncher Evans Coleman once remarked that he knew cowhands "who could neither read nor write, but who could name any brand, either letters or figures, on a cow." A brand was the key to ownership in a business where ownership was everything. Many cattlemen, in fact, named their ranches after their brands and held the symbol in as proud esteem as did any knight his crest. Branding was an ancient practice before the first cow

came to America. Certain 4,000-year-old tomb paintings show Egyptians branding their fat, spotted cattle. Hernando Cortés burned crosses on the hides of the small herd he brought with him to Mexico. The vaqueros passed the custom on to U.S. cowboys, who developed and refined their own calligraphy.

On any 19th Century ranch the greenest cowhand quickly mastered the three major elements of the brand-

ing alphabet (below). He learned to read the components of a brand in correct order: from left to right, from top to bottom, or from outside to inside (a T inside a diamond translates as Diamond T, not T Diamond). In time he could pick out any one of hundreds of markings in a milling herd; a good cowboy, said Coleman, could understand "the Constitution of the United States were it written with a branding iron on the side of a cow."

THE COWBOY'S CRYPTIC ALPHABET

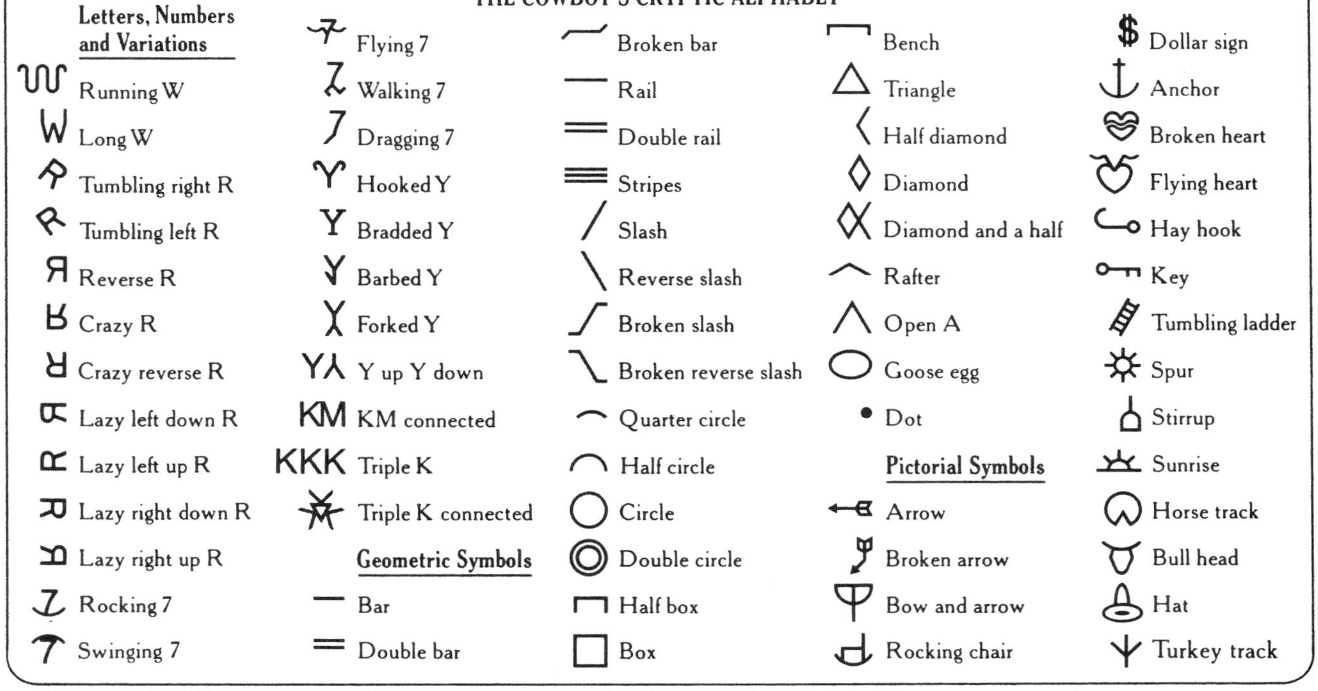

Letters, Numbers and Variations

ɰ	Running W	
W	Long W	
⋔	Tumbling right R	
⋌	Tumbling left R	
Я	Reverse R	
Ʀ	Crazy R	
ᴚ	Crazy reverse R	
⊡	Lazy left down R	
⊡	Lazy left up R	
⊐	Lazy right down R	
⊐	Lazy right up R	
⫦	Rocking 7	
⌅	Swinging 7	

⇁	Flying 7
�ↄ	Walking 7
7	Dragging 7
Υ	Hooked Y
Y	Bradded Y
Ψ	Barbed Y
X	Forked Y
YΛ	Y up Y down
KM	KM connected
KKK	Triple K
Ҝ	Triple K connected

Geometric Symbols

—	Bar
⹀	Double bar

⌒	Broken bar
—	Rail
═	Double rail
≡	Stripes
/	Slash
\	Reverse slash
⟋	Broken slash
\	Broken reverse slash
⌒	Quarter circle
⌣	Half circle
○	Circle
◎	Double circle
⊓	Half box
☐	Box

⌐	Bench
△	Triangle
⟨	Half diamond
◇	Diamond
⟨X⟩	Diamond and a half
⌒	Rafter
∧	Open A
○	Goose egg
•	Dot

Pictorial Symbols

⟵	Arrow
⟱	Broken arrow
Ψ	Bow and arrow
⟱	Rocking chair

$	Dollar sign
⚓	Anchor
♡	Broken heart
♡	Flying heart
⌐	Hay hook
⊶	Key
⌸	Tumbling ladder
☼	Spur
⌂	Stirrup
⚕	Sunrise
⌒	Horse track
⩒	Bull head
⌂	Hat
⋎	Turkey track

FOUR TYPICAL BRANDS AND WHAT THEY MEAN

Monogram

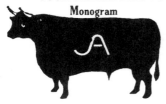

Charles Goodnight's simple and famous J A brand spells out the initials of his partner John Adair. The running curves have a practical purpose: sharp angles tend to blotch and blur the brand.

Phonogram

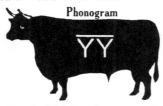

Rancher J. H. Barwise re-created the two syllables of his last name in symbolic equivalents that combine to form his brand. Read correctly from top to bottom, this puzzle works out as Bar Ys.

Pictograph

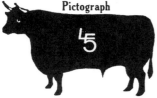

A gunslinger turned rancher arrived in the West with nothing but two .45-caliber pistols to his name. Later, when he made good as a cattleman, those two guns were memorialized in his brand.

Word Story

"A man's a fool to raise cattle," said Texan T. J. Walker, and he took the word for his brand. Fun-loving cowpunchers with running irons would sometimes rope his bulls and change the F to a B.

Cowboys dispute a cattle brand

Cowgirl Poetry by Reine River

NINE SORREL HORSES

You gave me your wild rag
With nine Sorrel horses
It's worn and it's torn
And it was once your protection
Those nine Sorrel horses, I think
Could be missin' you
Kind of in the same way
My heart keeps thinkin', thinkin' of you
My Nevada buckaroo

Their big brown eyes, look straight at me you see
Their thoughts are ponderin', about you and me
They lie still on my bed
They feel soft to my touch
but they're missin' your sparks
I'm afraid they lie buried, awaitin' your touch

I caress those nine Sorrel horses
and remember the times, stories, and laughter,
And the love we once shared

You are a long ways from here
And your wild rag is here
It's what's left of your memory
And I'm craving it, dear

If I could I would choose one
The fastest one
I would ride the best Sorrel
Of the nine that are there

Then I would attach your braided blizzard string
The one that you gave me the last time I was there
To the hat that would cover
And protect my head fierce
And set my vision to the man I love dear

Now the only thing left is my heart, that is true
And the only protection is your love, when I'm there
I will wear your old rag
It will carry me through
I will ride up to you
And those nine Sorrel horses
Will be restin' nearby
They'll be lyin' on your bed, this time
And I, will be at your side

copyright (c) 1988 Reine River

CHAMPAGNE BANDANNA

Pewter frame champagne bandanna
The mixin's of a troubled thought
Dust and dirt, and the wind blows hard
The earth smells of burnin' cattle fur
Pewter frame champagne bandanna
Takes me back to Jiggs, Nevada

A bed of cows drift through a basin
The clatter of hoofs leave dust a shakin'
Oh pewter frame champagne bandanna
Makes me think of Jiggs, Nevada

I remember the smell
The cries of cattle
Dehornin' and blood seemed everywhere
The click of my camera
His rope soars high
A steer is pulled
And more brandin' takes place
That steer cries his last bull cry
Pewter frame champagne Bandanna
Takes me back to Jiggs, Nevada

Deep in dust
The wind blows harder
More cattle wrestle beneath my feet
I hear a moanin' cry above
I remember it well
That day in Nevada

To look at you now
In a pewter frame champagne bandanna
I remember the man
I thought I knew so well

Pewter frame champagne bandanna
Won't you take me back to Jiggs, Nevada

Copyright (c) 1988 Reine River

RIGHT ABOUT NOW

There's always a snake
That passes me by
He'll move slowly and quietly
Right by my side

He'll slither one way
An' back down the other
While he'll be up an' about
B'fore I can holler

There's always a snake
He'll rattle an' slide
Up along your backside

I've laid down beside him
I've held him an' kissed him
But be careful around him
He'll swallow you whole

He'll tell you he loves you
An' wants you beside him
He'll rub up against you
Caress you an' press you

There's always a snake
An' make no mistake
He'll give you sweet kisses
An' oh so sweet an' so quick
His tougue can be swift

He'll tell you he loves you
All through the night
He'll get up
An' then right about now
whooooaaa
Be carefull for his bite can be deadly
An' in spite of all that
Why he's just an ol' snake
An' he knows better than that

Copyright (c) 1988 Reine River

Reine River has a Cassette tape of her Cowgirl poetry set to music,
"Buckin' Heart"
P. O. Box 26774
Los Angeles, CA 90026

Billy The Kid

William Bonney, born in New York City in 1859. By the time he was eighteen he was a murderer, at nineteen, he had a reputation as a cold-blooded killer. At twenty-one he was the scourge of New Mexico. And then he was dead, shot to death by Sheriff Pat Garrett on July 14, 1881, in Fort Sumner, New Mexico. Billy was a cruel and blood-thirsty killer, who cast a ghastly shadow over his time and place. This song was composed long after Bonney's death.

I'll sing you a true song of Bil - ly the Kid, I'll

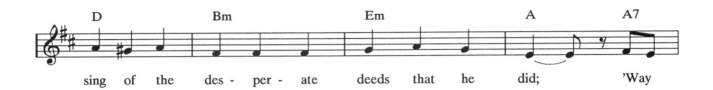

sing of the des - per - ate deeds that he did; 'Way

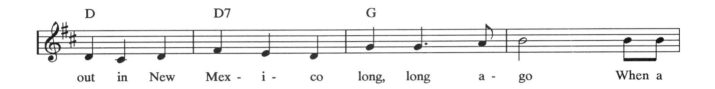

out in New Mex - i - co long, long a - go When a

man's on - ly chance was his own for - ty - four.

'Twas on the same night that poor Billy died,
He said to his friends, 'I'm not satisfied;
There are twenty-one men I've put bullets through,
And Sheriff Pat Garrett must make twenty-two.'

Now this is how Billy the Kid met his fate,
The bright moon was shining, the hour was late;
Shot down by Pat Garrett who once was his friend,
The young outlaw's life had come to its end.

There's many a man with face fine and fair,
Who starts out in life with a chance to be square;
But just like poor Billy, he wanders astray.
And loses his life the very same way.

I'll sing you a true song of Billy the Kid,
I'll sing of the desperate deeds that he did;
'Way out in New Mexico long, long ago,
When a man's only chance was his old forty-four.

When Billy the Kid was a very young lad,
In old Silver City, he went to the bad;
Way out in the West with a gun in his hand,
At the age of twelve years he killed his first man.

Fair Mexican maidens play guitars and sing,
A song about Billy, their boy bandit king;
How, ere his young manhood had reached its sad end,
Had a notch on his pistol for twenty-one men.

Pat Garrett's fanciful farewell to the Kid

The original cover of the Garrett opus

The legend that grew up around Billy the Kid had many promoters, but none more unlikely than Sheriff Pat Garrett, the man who did him in. Soon after shooting the young killer in July 1881, Garrett teamed up with an itinerant journalist, Ashmun Upson, to produce *An Authentic Life of Billy the Kid.* The preface declared loftily: "I am incited to this labor by an impulse to correct the thousand false statements which have appeared in the public newspapers and in yellow-covered cheap novels."

In fact, the book, while accurately illustrated, was as careless with the truth as the dime novels Garrett purported to despise. For example, Billy did not, at the age of 12, kill a loafer because the man insulted his mother — or for any other reason. Nor did he rescue a wagon train by routing Indian attackers with an ax, or ride 81 miles in six hours to spring a friend from a Texas jail. Yet, since such tales were printed under the byline of the Kid's nemesis, many readers came to accept them as gospel.

Garrett's own reputation suffered no harm from these fictional touches. Already famed throughout the Southwest, he went on to serve as a captain in the Texas Rangers and win an appointment as a customs collector from President Teddy Roosevelt — whom he had met at a luncheon in San Antonio. But when a New Mexico ranch he had purchased began to fail, Garrett became a morose fixture in saloons. Finally, in 1908, he was killed by a neighbor after a protracted feud — an ironic end for a man who, in his book, had claimed responsibility for bringing New Mexico "a season of peace and prosperity to which she has ever, heretofore, been a stranger."

Trapped in a cabin, the Kid and his rustler cohorts signal surrender after one outlaw and a horse are killed by Sheriff Garett's possemen.

Billy fells a deputy with a shotgun blast from the balcony of the Lincoln County jail prior to his final escape from the clutches of the law

Entering Pete Maxwell's darkened bedroom. Billy is surprised by Garrett and brought down with a bullet to the heart without returning fire.

Tex Ritter

Bar D Wranglers

Blue Mountain

Drifting from ranch to ranch, owning nothing except a cow pony, saddle, and "hot roll," the cowboys rode the "chuck line"-begged, that is-from ranch to ranch, staying out their welcome at each before moving on. This song expresses the cowboy image of being on the "chuck line."

My home it was in Texas,
My past you must not know;
I seek a refuge from the law
Where the sage and pinon grow.

CHORUS:
Blue Mountain, you're azure deep,
Blue Mountain, with sides so steep,
Blue Mountain with horse head on your side,
You have won my love to keep.

For the brand 'LC' I ride,
And the sleeper calves on the side,
I'll own the 'Hip-Side-and-Shoulder' when I grow older,
Zapitaro, don't tan my hide!

I chum with Latigo Gordon,
I drink at the Blue Goose saloon,
I dance at night with the Mormon girls,
And ride home beneath the moon .

I trade at Mons' store
With bullet holes in the door;
His calico treasure my horse can measure
When I'm drunk and feeling sore.

Yarn Gallus with shortened lope
Doc Few-Clothes without any soap,
In the little green valley have made their sally,
And for Slicks there's still some hope.

In the summer time it's fine,
In the winter the wind doth whine,
But say, dear brother, if you want a mother,
There's Ev on the old chuck line.

The Colorado Trail

The Colorado Trail left the trunk line of the Western Trail in southern Oklahoma and angled off to the northwest through the Texas Panhandle and into Colorado. In Colorado the trail crossed Two Butte Creek and the Purgatorie River ending in La Junta. Long trail driving days and the feelings of a lovesick cowboy are both here in this herding song.

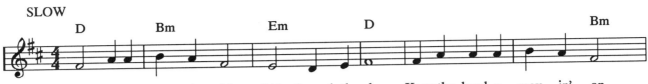

Ride all the lone-ly night, Ride through the day. Keep the herd a-mov-in' on,

CHORUS

Mov-in' on its way. Weep all ye lit-tle rains, Wail, winds, ___ wail.

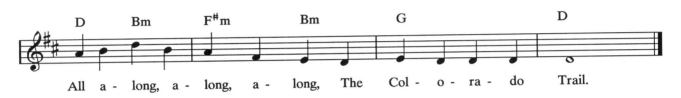

All a-long, a-long, a-long, The Col-o-ra-do Trail.

1. Ride all the lonely night,
   Ride through the day.
   Keep the herd a-movin' on,
   Movin' on its way.

   Chorus
   Weep all ye little rains,
   Wail, winds, wail.
   All along, along, along,
   The Colorado Trail.

2. Eyes like the morning star,
   Cheeks like a rose.
   Laura was a pretty girl,
   God Almighty knows.

   Chours

3. Ride through the stormy night,
   Dark is the sky.
   Wish I'd stayed in Abilene,
   Nice and warm and dry.

   Chorus

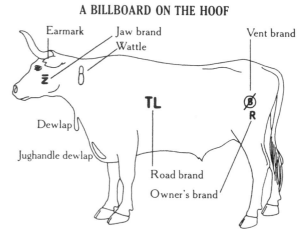

A BILLBOARD ON THE HOOF

A range cow was often a walking billboard of marks from hot irons and sharp knives. These marks could appear almost anywhere on the animal, but the locations shown here were common. From its first owner it often got a hip brand (and a jaw brand if the original was unclear or incorrect). A trail driver later marked its side with a road brand. A subsequent purchaser might mark out (or vent) the old hip brand and burn his own nearby. Since brands were hard to read in herds, cattle also bore knife cuts (wattles, dewlaps or earmarks) on their necks, throats, briskets and ears.

Igor's Cowboy Jazz Band

Cowboy's Gettin' Up Holler

The cowboy was up at the crack of dawn, but the camp cook was up even earlier, making the fire, putting up the coffee, baking his hoecakes. It was a tough, long job, and under difficult conditions. .A good cook earned his comparatively handsome pay. You can sing this with out rhythm

1. Wake up, Ja - cob, Day's a - break - in', _____

Peas in the pot and the hoe-cake's bak-in'! _ ear-ly in the morn-ing, Al-most day,_ If you

don't come soon, Gon-na throw it all a-way. _ (Hit on pan) Wake up!

Wake up, Jacob,
Day's a-breakin',
Peas in the pot
And the hoecake's bakin'!

Early in the morning,
Almost day,
If you don't come soon,
Gonna throw it all away.

Wake up, Jacob!
Bacon in the pan,
Coffee in the pot,
Get up and get it—
Get it while it's hot.

> *It was chuck-time on the round up, and we heard "Old Doughy shout*
> *"You had better come and get this or I"ll throw the whole thing out."*
> *So we headed for the wagon like a wild stampeded herd.*
> *Fearful every minute lest the cook might keep his word.*

Wyoming State Archives, Museums and Historical Department

FOUR DISTINCTIVE STYLES IN COWBOY HEADGEAR

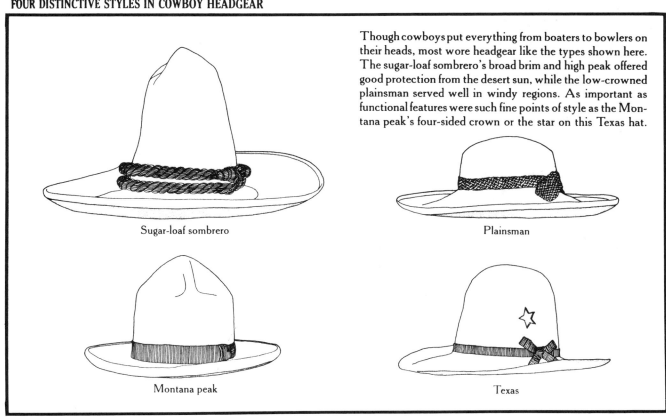

Though cowboys put everything from boaters to bowlers on their heads, most wore headgear like the types shown here. The sugar-loaf sombrero's broad brim and high peak offered good protection from the desert sun, while the low-crowned plainsman served well in windy regions. As important as functional features were such fine points of style as the Montana peak's four-sided crown or the star on this Texas hat.

Sugar-loaf sombrero

Plainsman

Montana peak

Texas

The Cowboy's Ride

For sheer lyricism this song is hard to beat, we sense behind it a poet inspired both by the prairies of the West and the Anglo-American literary heritage.

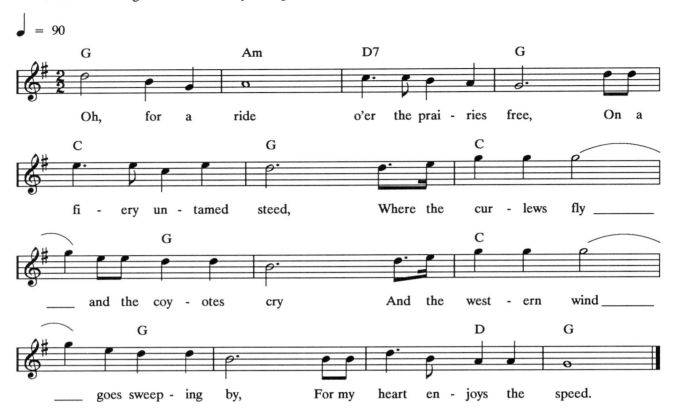

♩ = 90

Oh, for a ride o'er the prai - ries free, On a fi - ery un - tamed steed, Where the cur - lews fly ____ ____ and the coy - otes cry And the west - ern wind _____ ____ goes sweep - ing by, For my heart en - joys the speed.

Oh, for a ride o'er the prairies free,
On a fiery untamed steed,
Where the curlews fly and the coyotes cry
And the western wind goes sweeping by,
For my heart enjoys the speed.

With my left hand light on the bridle rein,
And saddle girth pinched behind,
With a lariat tied at the pony's side
By my stout right arm that's true and tried,
We race with the whistling wind.

We're up and away in the morning light
As swift as a shooting star,
That suddenly files across the sky,
And the wild birds whirl in quick surprise
At the cowboy's gay 'Hurrah!'

As free as a bird o'er the rolling sea
We skim the pasture wide,
Like a seagull strong we hurry along,
And the earth resounds with a galloping song
As we sail through the fragrant tide.

You can have your ride in the crowded town!
Give me the prairies free.
Where the curlews fly and the coyotes cry,
And the heart expands 'neath the open sky:
Oh, that's the ride for me!

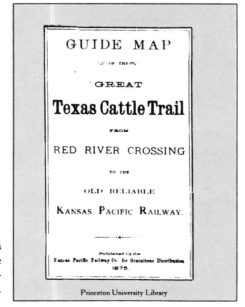

GUIDE MAP

OF THE

GREAT

Texas Cattle Trail

FROM

RED RIVER CROSSING

TO THE

OLD RELIABLE

KANSAS PACIFIC RAILWAY.

Published by the
Kansas Pacific Railway Co. for Gratuitous Distribution.
1875.

Princeton University Library

Before starting on the long drives, cattle bosses picked up handy trail guides offered free by the various Western railroads as a means of promoting their profitable beef-hauling business.

The Cowboy's Lament

Also known as "The Streets Of Laredo," Written by Francis Henry Maynard in 1876 in Tom Sherman's barroom in Dodge City, Kansas. It has been adapted to fit two locales, one in Dodge City and the other is the streets of Laredo, Texas. Sung everywhere on the trail and the range, and is still one of the favorite songs of today.

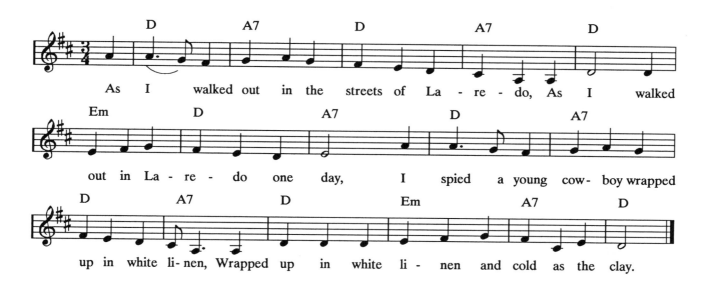

As I walked out in the streets of La - re - do, As I walked out in La - re - do one day, I spied a young cow- boy wrapped up in white li- nen, Wrapped up in white li - nen and cold as the clay.

1. As I walked out in the streets of Laredo,
   As I walked out in Laredo one day,
   I spied a young cowboy wrapped up in white linen,
   Wrapped up in white linen and cold as the clay.

2. 'O beat the drum slowly and pla the fife lowly;
   Play the Dead March as you carry me along.
   Take me to the green valley and lay the sod o'er me,
   For I'm a young cowboy and I know I've done wrong.'

3. 'I see by your outfit that you are a cowboy.'
   These words he did say as I boldly stepped by.
   'Come sit down beside me and hear my sad story;
   I'm shot in the breast and I know I must die.'

4. 'My friends and relations they live in the Nation;
   They know not where their dear boy has gone.
   I first came to Taxas and hired to a ranchman,
   O I'm a young cowboy and I know I've done wrong.'

5. 'It was once in the saddle I used to go dashing;
   It was once in the saddle I used to go gay.
   First to the dram house and then to the card house,
   Got shot in the breast and I'm dying today.'

6. 'Get six jolly cowboys to carry my coffin;
   Get six pretty maidens to bear up my pall.
   Put bunches of roses all over my coffin,
   Put roses to deaden the clods as they fall.'

7. 'Go gather around you a group of young cowboys,
   And tell them the story of this my sad fate.
   Tell one and the other, before they go further,
   To stop their wild roving before it's too late.'

8. 'Go bring me a cup, a cup of cold water
   To cool my parched lips,' the young cowboy said.
   Before I returned, the spirit had left him
   And gone to its Maker - the cowboy was dead.

9. We beat the drum slowly and played the fife lowly,
   And bitterly wept as we bore him along.
   For we all loved our comrade, so brave, young, and handsome,
   We all loved our comrade although he'd done wrong.

53

Doney Gal

A night herding song and one of the best about a cowboy's horse. Doney Gal meant sweetheart. Often the name of a favorite girl was used for a favorite horse, I wonder how the girls felt about that? Play this one slow. Alan Lomax believes that it is one of the last of the genuine cowboy songs.

We're a-lone, Don-ey Gal, in the wind and hail. Got-ta drive these do-gies down the trail.

We ride the range from sun to sun, For a cow-boy's work is nev-er done.

We're up and gone at the break of day Driv-ing the do-gies on their wea-ry way.

It's rain or shine, sleet or snow, Me and my Don-ey Gal are bound to go.

Yes, rain or shine, sleet or snow, Me and my Don-ey Gal are on the go.

Prelude
> We're alone, Doney Gal, in the wind and hail.
> Gotta drive these dogies down the trail.

1. We ride the range from sun to sun,
   For a cowboy's work is never done.
   We're up and gone at the break of day
   Driving the dogies on their weary way.

Chorus
> It's rain or shine, sleet or snow,
> Me and my Doney Gal are bound to go.
> Yes, rain or shine, sleet or snow,
> Me and my Doney Gal are on the go.

2. A cowboy's life is a dreary thing,
   For it's rope, and brand, and ride, and sing.
   Yes, day or night in rain or hail,
   We'll stay with the dogies on the trail.

   Chorus

3. We travel down that lonesome trail,
   Where a man and his horse seldom ever fail.
   We laugh at storms, sleet, and snow,
   When we camp near San Antonio.

   Chorus

4. Tired and hungry, far from home,
   I'm just a poor cowboy and bound to roam.
   Starless nights and lightning glare,
   Danger and darkness every where.

   Chorus

5. Drifting my Doney Gal round and round,
   Steers are asleep on a new bed ground.
   Riding night herd all night long,
   Singing softly a cowboy song.

   Chorus

6. Swimming rivers along the way,
   Pushing for the North Star day by day.
   Storm clouds break, and at breakneck speed
   We follow the steers in a wild stampede.

   Chorus

7. Over the praires lean and brown
   And on through wastes where there ain't no town.
   Bucking dust storms, wind, and hail,
   Pushing the longhorns up the trail.

   Chorus

8. Trailing the herd through mountains green,
   We pen all the cattle at Abilene.
   Then round the campfire's flickering glow
   We sing the songs of long ago.

   Chorus

"Dude" Mouron

Don Edwards

Reinsmen

The Girl That Wore A Waterfall

Cowboys, especially the younger ones reared on the range, were an easy touch for gamblers and prostitutes when they did get to town. Witness the disgrace of the young cowboy in this song. Beauty was only skin deep! A waterfall was a roll of hair worn low on the neck, or a hat with a long, drooping feather in back.

Come all young men who've been in love and sympathize with me, For I have loved as fair a maid as ever you did see. Her age it was but seventeen, a figure fair and tall, She was a handsome creature and she wore a waterfall.

Come all young men who've been in love and sympathize with me,
For I have loved as fair a maid as ever you did see.
Her age it was but seventeen, a figure far and tall,
She was a handsome creature and she wore a waterfall.

The first time that I met her, I never shall forget,
I'd slipped into a dry goods store some handkerchiefs to get.
She stood behind the counter dressed up just like a doll,
I never saw a face so fair or such a waterfall.

'Twas at a picnic party, I met her after that,
I quickly introduced myself; we had a pleasant chat.
Though many other girls were there, yet none of them at all
Could dance with me except the girl who wore the waterfall.

I saw her home, we marched along, we said we'd never part,
And when she asked me to come in I found I'd lost my heart;
While sitting there I thought I heard some footsteps in the hall,
All sorts of colors turned the girl who wore the waterfall.

A great big fellow six feet high came stalking in the room,
And when he saw me sitting there at once began to fume.
His eyes so hard, his face so harsh, it did my heart appall-
'This is my husband,' said the girl who wore the waterfall.

Before I'd time to say a word the fellow at me flew,
And while the maiden held me down he beat me black and blue.
When I got up I found I'd lost watch, money, chain and all-
I never since go near a girl who wears a waterfall.

Git Along Little Dogies

This slow jogging song just fit the trail driving conditions and moods of the drive. At times intense and thrilling but mostly it was pretty routine.

As I walked out one morn - ing for pleas - ure, I met a cow - punch - er a - jog - ging a - long; His hat was thrown back and his spurs was a - jing - ling, And as he ad - vanced he was sing - ing this song: _____ 'Sing hoop - li - o, _____ get a - long my lit - tle do - gies, For Wy - o - ming shall be your new home. It's __ hoop - ing and yell - ing and curs - ing those do - gies To our mis - for - tune but none of your own.' _____

As I walked out one morning for pleasure,
    I met a cowpuncher a-jogging along;
His hat was thrown back and his spurs was a-jingling,
    And as he advanced he was singing this song -

CHORUS

    'Sing hooplio, get along my little dogies,
        For Wyoming shall be your new home.
    It's hooping and yelling and cursing those dogies
        To our misfortune but none of your own.'

In the Springtime we round up the dogies,
    Slap on the brands and bob off their tails;
Then we cut herd and herd is inspected,
    And then we throw them on the trail.

In the evening we round in the dogies
    As they are grazing from herd all around.
You have no idea the trouble they give us
    As we are holding them on the bedground.

In the morning we throw off the bedground,
    Aiming to graze them an hour or two.
When they are full, you think you can drive them
    On the trail, but be damned if you do.

Some fellows go on the trail for pleasure,
    But they have got this thing down wrong;
If it hadn't been for these troublesome dogies,
    I never would thought of writing this song.

Courtesy, Archives Division, Texas State Library

Green Grow The Lilacs

An old Irish song, widely popular with the early Texas Cowboys. A colorful fable holds that the Mexican word "gringo." meaning cowboy, was derived from the song, for the Mexicans referred to the Americans by the first two words of the title "Green Grow," pronouncing it "*Gringo*." True or not, it makes a good story.

Green grow the li - lacs, all spark - ling with dew, I'm
lone - ly, my dar - ling, since part - ing with you. But
by our next meet - ing I'll hope to prove true, And
change the green li - lacs to the Red, White and Blue.

1. Green grow the lilacs, sparkling with dew,
   I'm lonely, my darling, since parting with you.
   But by our next meeting I'll hope to prove true,
   And change the green lilacs to the Red, White and Blue.

2. I used to have a sweetheart, but now I have none,
   Since she's gone and left me, I care not for one.
   Since she's gone and left me, contented I'll be,
   For she loves another one better than me.

3. I passed my love's window, both early and late,
   The look that she gave me, it made my heart ache.
   Oh, the look that she gave me was painful to see,
   For she loves another one better than me.

4. I wrote my love letters in rosy red lines,
   She sent me an answer all twisted in twines,
   Saying, 'Keep your love letters and I will keep mine,
   Just you write to your love and I'll write to mine.'

5. Green grow the lilacs, all sparkling with dew,
   I'm lonely, my darling, since parting with you,
   But by our next meeting I'll hope to prove true,
   And change the green lilacs to Red, White and Blue.

Angora

60

THE ELEMENTS OF A CATCH ROPE

For ordinary roundup work like calf catching most American cowboys used a grass rope averaging 40 feet in length. At the head of the lariat was an eyelet called a honda, through which the main line of the rope slid to form a loop usually four feet or more in diameter. To toss the lariat, a cowboy grasped both the main line and the loop in his throwing hand (*as at right*), with the honda about a quarter of the way down the loop for balance. In his other hand he held the coiled remainder of the rope, letting out extra line with his thumb and index finger. The last two fingers of the same hand held the reins in order to guide the cow pony through the quick stops and turns of the roping sequence.

Two kinds of ropes and hondas

The lariat introduced by the vaqueros was made of braided rawhide and was so easy to throw that the average length for one was 60 feet. But it was expensive and a little delicate, and most Americans turned to tough grass. The grass rope was also more practical in that it could easily be knotted to form the honda, while rawhide usually had to be spliced around a piece of cowhorn.

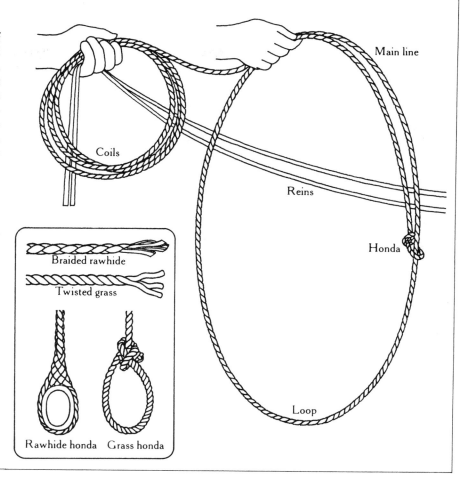

Braided rawhide

Twisted grass

Rawhide honda   Grass honda

Main line

Coils

Reins

Honda

Loop

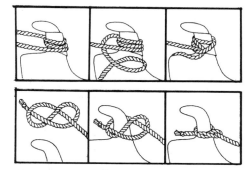

Dallying to hold a calf or steer

Men working in open country held a roped animal by taking a few turns, or dallies, around the saddle horn. When dismounting they locked the rope with a half hitch

Hard and fast for rough country

In brushy or rocky terrain, where a loosened dally might mean a lost calf, range hands kept the near ends of their ropes tied hard and fast with a figure-8 knot.

Charles M. Russell's The Virginian. *He rolled his own*

61

I Ride An Old Paint

1. I ride an old paint, I lead an old Dan.
   I'm off to Montan' for to throw the hoolihan.*
   They feed in the coulees, they water in the draw;
   Their tails are all matted, their backs are all raw.

Chorus
Ride around little dogies, ride around themslow,
For the fiery and snuffy are a-rarin' to go.

*bulldogging,
*a roping term, a quick throw with a small loop,
*or to "paint the town red".

2. Old Bill Jones had two daughters and a song,
   One went to Denver, and the other went wrong.
   His wife, she died in a poolroom fight,
   And he sings this song from morning till night.

Chorus

3. O when I die, take my saddle from the wal,
   Put it on my pony and lead him from the stall
   Tie my bones to his back, turn our faces to the west,
   And we'll ride the prairies we love the best.

Chorus

Jesse James

Was Jesse James the Robin Hood of America? Well a dozen different ballads exalt him as such. For fifteen years the notorious James brothers reigned as the scourge of Kansas and Missouri. Jesse, the younger of the two, became the colorful mastermind and daring desperado of the gang. In April of 1882, Jesse was murdered by Robert Ford, one of his trusted gunmen, for the reward of $10,000. Ten years later Ford died at the hand of an assassin in a small Colorado town.

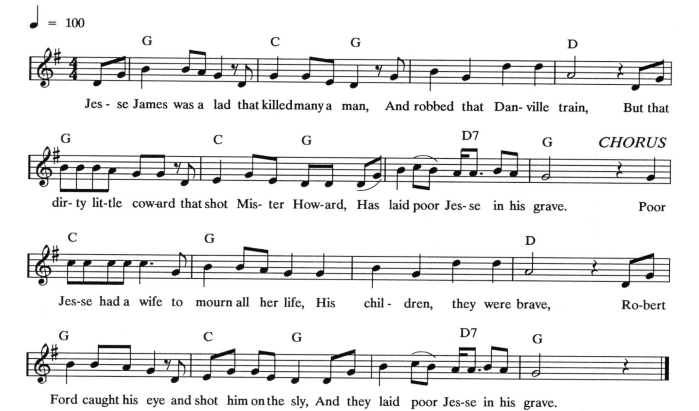

1. Jesse James was a lad that killed many a man,
   And robbed that Danville train,
   But that dirty little coward that shot Mister Howard,
   Has laid poor Jess in his grave.

   Poor Jesse had a wife to mourn all her life
   His children, they were brave,
   Robert Ford caught his eye and shot him on the sly,
   And they laid poor Jesse in his grave.

2. It was his brother Frank stuck up the Pittsfield Bank,
   And carried the money from the town,
   It was in this very place that they had a little race,
   For they shot Captain Sheets to the ground. *(Chorus)*

3. They went to the crossing not very far from there,
   And there they did the same,
   With the agent on his knees, he delivered up the keys,
   To the outlaws, Frank and Jesse James. *(Chorus)*

4. It was on a Wednesday night, the moon was shining bright,
   They stopped the Glendale train,
   He robbed from the rich and he gave to the poor,
   He'd a heart, and a hand and a brain. *(Chorus)*

5. It was on a Saturday night when Jesse was at home,
   Talking with his family brave,
   Robert Ford's pistol ball brought him tumbling from the wall
   And they laid poor Jesse in his grave. *(Chorus)*

6. It was Robert Ford, that dirty little coward,
   I wonder how he does feel,
   For he ate of Jesse's bread, and he slept in Jesse's bed,
   And then laid poor Jesse in his grave. *(Chorus)*

7. This song was made by Billy Gashade
   As soon as the news did arrive,
   He said there was no man with the law in his hand,
   Could take Jesse James when alive. *(Chorus)*

Still neophytes at banditry. Frank and Jesse James flaunt their long-barreled revolvers. Frank (left), the older by three years, was quiet and bookish, while Jesse, as a friend put it, was "reckless and devil-may-care".

Bob Ford shows off the pearl-handled .44 he used to dispatch Jesse James-originally a gift from the gang leader himself.

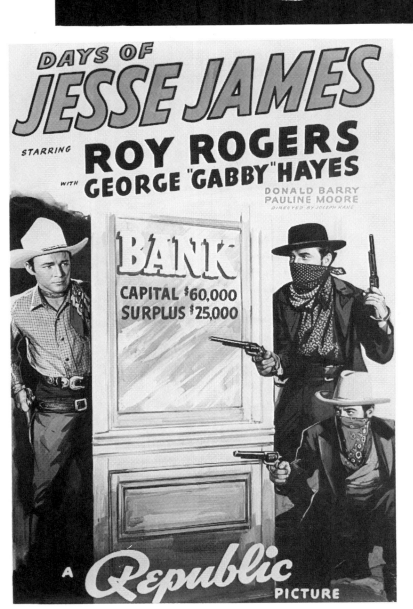

A model of youthful decorum, Jesse James seems a lad his Baptist-minster father would have been proud of-and even as an outlaw he retained a streak of piety.

In a scene from *Life and Times of Jesse and Frank James,* their men round up valuables from train passengers. The book's author said it had been dictated by Jesse's wife and mother, a claim both denied.

While most contemporary portrayals of the James gang's exploits embroidered the truth, this holdup, in Kentucky in 1880, took place as depicted. One stage passenger's watch was later recovered in Jesse's home.

An equally canny merchandiser of his past, Frank James — here a spry 70 — plays host at his birthplace. Tourists plunked down money not only to see the outlaw shrine but to buy pebbles from Jesse's grave.

The Lavender Cowboy

The title alone suggests a spoof on the tough hombres that myth insists the cowboys were.

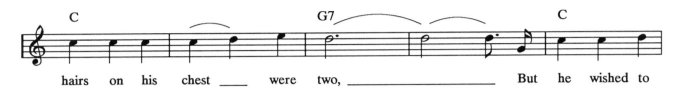

He was on - ly a lav - en - der cow - boy, _____ The

hairs on his chest ____ were two, _____ But he wished to

fol - low the he - roes _____ And fight like the

he - men ____ do. _____

He was only a lavender cowboy
  The hairs on his chest were two,
But he wished to follow the heroes
  And fight like the he-men do.

But he was inwardly troubled
  By a dream that gave him no rest,
That he'd go with heroes in action
  With only two hairs on his chest.

First he tried many a hair tonic,
  'Twar rubbed in on him each night,
But still when he looked in the mirror
  Those two hairs were ever in sight.

But with a spirit undaunted
  He wandered out to fight,
Just like an old-time knight errant
  To win combat for the right.

He battled for Red Nellie's honor
  And cleaned out a holdup's nest,
He died with his six guns a-smoking
  With only two hairs on his chest.

Lily Of The West

In the cowboy code true love is disquieting, unique, compulsive, everlasting. That the object thereof prove unworthy means nothing: the stricken lover still seeks her out, still loves and keeps hoping.

As I went down to Lou-is-ville some pleas-ure for to find,_____ There

came a girl from Lex-ing-ton so pleas-ing to my mind;_____ Her _

hair was laid in dia-monds and a star up-on her breast,_____ They

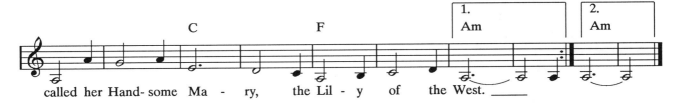

called her Hand-some Ma-ry, the Lil-y of the West._____

As I went down to Louisville some pleasure for to find,
There came a girl from Lexingtown so pleasing to my mind;
Her hair was laid in diamonds and a star upon her breast,
They called her Handsome Mary, the Lily of the West.

She had rings on every finger that come from the distant shores,
Ten thousand hundred dollars laid up for her in store;
'Tis enough to entice the king of Press, how costly she did dress,
And I called her my sweet Mary, the Lily of the West.

I courted her for a long time, her love I expected to gain,
Until she turned her back on to me and I to her the same;
But I never shall forget that day the clod lie on my breast
And I talked to my sweet Mary, the Lily of the West.

One day when I was a-walking down by the shady grove
There come a man from Lexingtown, come dashing with my love;
He sung a song most melodious, it did my soul depress,
And he called her his sweet Mary, the Lily of the West.

My rifle on my shoulder, my dagger in my hand,
I caught him by the collar while bold I bid him stand;
Me being mad and desperated, I quickly pierced his breast,
For talking to my Mary, the Lily of the West.

They took me to the Justice, he only but made my plea,
The jury found me innocent, the judges set me free.
And they did not say more or less
Begone you scornfulish Mary, the Lily of the West.

There was a man among them that was so honorable mean,
He had me bound down in iron chains and brought me back again;
They put me in the guard house, my life to explore,
There are spies at every window, boys, and six at every door.

I went around in the guard house, I surveyed it around and around,
I jumped out at one window and knocked five of them down;
The footmen and the horsemen they quickly followed me,
But I wheeled old Jack four times around and gained my liberty.

I've traveled through the westerns, I've traveled America through,
And a-many pretty cottage girl has come into my view;
But I never shall forget that day the clod lie on my breast
And I talked to my sweet Mary, the Lily of the West.

My Love Is A Rider

Also called "Bucking Broncho". One of the bawdiest of all cowboy songs, and a favorite song of the cowboys, its the lament of a maiden. Said my many to be written by Belle Starr, a notorious woman outlaw of Texas and Indian Territory.

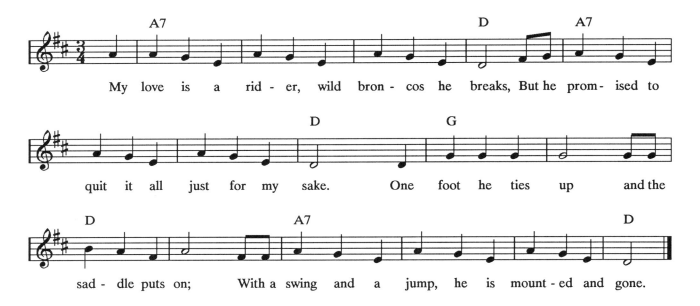

My love is a rid - er, wild bron - cos he breaks, But he prom - ised to

quit it all just for my sake. One foot he ties up and the

sad - dle puts on; With a swing and a jump, he is mount - ed and gone.

1. My love is a rider, wild broncos he breaks,
   But he promised to quit it all just for my sake.
   One foot he ties up and the saddle puts on;
   With a swing and a jump he is mounted and gone.

2. The first time I saw him was early one spring.
   He was riding a bronco, a high-headed thing.
   He tipped me a wink as he gaily did go,
   For he wished me to look at his bucking bronco.

3. The next time I saw him was late in the fall;
   He was swinging the ladies at Tomlinson's Hall.
   He laughed and we talked as we danced to and fro,
   And promised never to ride on another bronco.

4. He made me some presents, among them a ring.
   The thing that I gave him was a far better thing;
   'Twas a young maiden's heart, and I'll have you all know,
   He won it by riding his bucking bronco.

5. My love has a gun and that gun he can use.
   But he quit his gun fighting as well as his booze.
   He sold out his saddle, his spurs, and his rope,
   There's no more cowpunching, and that's what I hope.

6. My love has a gun that has gone to the bad,
   And that makes my lover feel pretty damned sad.
   For the gun it shoots high, and the gun it shoots low,
   And it wobbles around like a bucking bronco.

7. Now all you young maidens where ere you reside,
   Beware of the cowboy who swings the rawhide.
   He'll court you, and pet you, and leave you and go
   A-riding the trails on his bucking bronco.

Night Herding Song

Range cattle on a strange bed-ground are as nervous as a cat in a room full of rocking chairs. They sniff and pace and mill, and any sudden noise may set off a stampede. The night herding cowboys on duty keep up a constant clucking, whistling, crooning and singing to the rhythm of their walking horse, to quiet the cattle, as well as to keep themselves from dozing in the saddle. This song appealing to those restless little dogies, is one of the more beautiful ones.

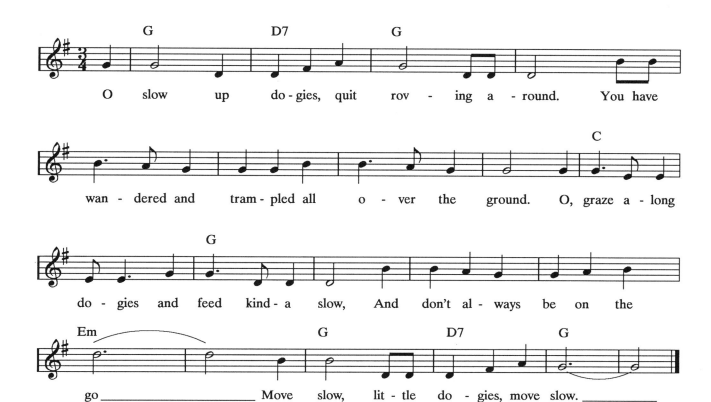

1. O slow up dogies, quit roving around.
   You have wandered and trampled all over the ground.
   O, graze along dogies and feed kinda slow.
   And don't always be on the go -
   Move slow, little dogies, move slow.

2. I've circle-herded, trail-herded, night-herded too.
   But to keep you together is all I can do.
   My horse is leg-weary and I'm awful tired,
   If you get away, I will be fired -
   Bunch up, little dogies, bunch up

3. O, say little dogies, when you gonna lay down,
   And quit this forever a-shifting around?
   My limbs are weary and my seat is all sore,
   Lay down like you've laid down before -
   Lay down, little dogies, lay down.

4. Lay still little dogies, since you have laid down.
   And stretch away out on the big, open ground.
   Snore loud little dogies, and drown the wild sound
   That'll leave when the day rolls around -
   Lay still, little dogies, lay still.

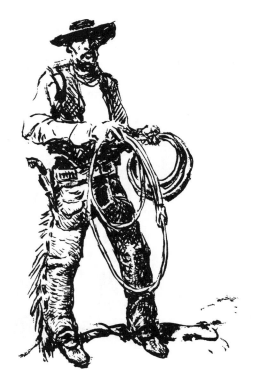

Closed leg

No Use for the Women

A cowboy brooding over the fate of a buddy who lost in love, fell in with evil companions, killed a gambler, gunned down by lawmen and buried out on the prairie. The whole tragedy rests on an insult to the picture of the girl worshipped by the cowboy, maybe Lou deceive the cowboy? Also well known as "Bury Me Out On The Prairie.

Now I've got no use ____ for wom - en, _____ A true one may
nev - er be found; _____ They use a man for his mon - ey, ____ When it's
gone they'll turn him down. _____ They're all a - like at the
bot - tom, _____ Self - ish and grasp - ing for all _____ They'll stick by a
man while he's win - ning, _____ And laugh in his face at his fall. _____

70

Now I've got no use for women,
    A true one may never be found;
They use a man for his money,
    When it's gone they'll turn him down.
They're all alike at the bottom,
    Selfish and grasping for all,
They'll stick by a man while he's winning
    And laugh in his face at his fall.

My pal was an honest young puncher,
    Honest, upright and true;
But he turned to a hard shooting gunman
    On account of a girl named Lou.
He fell in with evil companions,
    The kind that are better off dead;
When a gambler insulted her picture
    He filled him full of lead.

All through the long night they trailed him,
    Through mesquite and thick chaparral;
And I couldn't help think of the woman
    As I saw him pitch and fall.
If she'd been the pal that she should have
    He might have been raising a son,
Instead of out there on the prairie,
    To die by the ranger's gun.

Death's sharp sting did not trouble,
    His chances for life were too slim;
But where they were putting his body
    Was all that worried him.
He lifted his head on his elbow,
    The blood from his wounds flowed red,
He gazed at his pals grouped around him
    As he whispered to them and said:

'Oh, bury me out on the prairie
    Where the coyotes may howl o'er my grave;
Bury me out on the prairie,
    But from them my bones please save.
Wrap me up in a blanket
    And bury me deep in the ground,
Cover me over with boulders
    Of granite, gray and round.'

So we buried him out on the prairie,
    Where the coyotes can howl o'er his grave,
And his soul is now a-resting
    From the unkind cut she gave,
And many another young puncher
    As he rides past that pile of stones,
Recalls some similar woman
    And envies his mouldering bones.

O Bury Me Not On The Lone Prairie

A song about the last wishes of a dying cowboy, is an adaptation of a poem about a burial at sea. One of the best known of all cowboy songs and known around the world, and among Americans it is a traditional western standard. Closely related in words and melody to "Carry Me Back to the Lone Prairie".

'O bur-y me not ____ on the lone prai-rie.' ____ These words came low _____

____ and mourn-ful-ly, _____ From the pal-lid lips ____ of a youth who

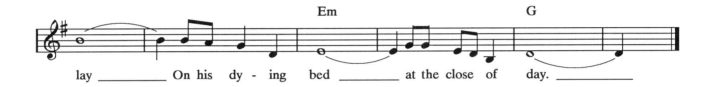

lay _____ On his dy-ing bed _____ at the close of day. _____

1. 'O bury me not on the lone prairie.'
    These words came low and mournfully,
  From the pallid lips of a youth who lay
    On his dying bed at the close of day.

2. He had wasted and pined till o'er his brow
    Death's shades were slowly gathering now.
  He thought of home and loved ones nigh,
    As the cowboys gathered to see him die.

3. 'O bury me not on the lone prairie,
    Where the coyotes howl and the wind blows free.
  In a narrow grave just six by three -
    O bury me not on the lone prairie.'

4. 'It matters not, I've oft been told,
    Where the body lies when the heart grows cold.
  Yet grant, o grant, this wish to me,
    O bury me not on the lone prairie.'

5. 'I've always wished to be laid when I died
    In a little churchyard on the green hillside.
  By my father's grave there let me be,
    O bury me not on the lone prairie.'

6. 'I wish to lie where a mother's prayer
    And a sister's tear will mingle there.
  Where friends can come and weep o'er me.
    O bury me not on the lone prairie.'

7. 'For there's another whose tears will shed
    For the one who lies in a prairie bed.
  It breaks my heart to think of her now,
    She has curled these locks; she has kissed this brow.'

8. 'O bury me not...' And his voice failed there
    But they took no heed to his dying prayer.
  In a narrow grave, just six by three,
    They buried him there on the lone prairie.

9. And the cowboys now as they roam the plain,
    For they marked the spot where his bones were lain,
  Fling a handful of roses o'er his grave
    With a prayer to God, his soul to save.

Sons Of The San Joaquin

Jim Bob Tinsley

Vince Lara

Mike Mahaney

Muzzie Braun and the Little Braun Brothers

The Old Chisholm Trail

The Chisholm Trail ran for a thousand miles from San Antonio into Montana and Wyoming, and said to be a stanza for every mile of the way.

Oh come a-long boys, and lis-ten to my tale, I'll

tell you all my troub-les on the ol' Chis'-m trail. Come a-

ti - yi - you - py you - py ya you - py yay, Come a-

ti yi you - py you - py yay.

Oh come along, boys, and listen to my tale,
I'll tell you all my troubles on the ol' Chis'm trail.

CHORUS
Come a-ti yi youpy youpy ya youpy yay,
Come a-ti yi youpy youpy yay.

On a ten-dollar horse and a forty-dollar saddle,
I was ridin', and a-punchin' Texas cattle.

We left ol' Texas October twenty-third,
Drivin' up trail with a 2 U Herd.

I'm up in the mornin' afore daylight,
An' afore I sleep the moon shines bright.

It's bacon and beans most every day,
I'd as soon be eatin' prairie hay.

Old Ben Bolt was a blamed good boss,
But he'd go to see the girls on a sore-backed hoss.

Old Ben Bolt was a mighty good man,
And you'd know there was whisky wherever he'd land.

I woke up one mornin' on the Chisholm trail,
With a rope in my hand and a cow by the tal.

Last night on guard, an' the leader broke the ranks,
I hit my horse down the shoulders an' spurred him
in the flanks.

Oh, it's cloudy in the west, and a-lookin' like rain,
And my damned ol' slicker's in the wagon again.

Oh the wind commenced to blow and the rain began to fall,
An' it looked by grab that we was gonna lose 'em all.

I jumped in the saddle an' I grabbed a-holt the horn,
The best damned cowpuncher ever was born.

I was on my best horse, and a-goin' on the run,
The quickest-shootin' cowboy that ever pulled a gun.

No chaps, no slicker, and it's pourin' down rain,
An' I swear, by God, I'll never nightherd again.

I herded and I hollered, and I done pretty well,
Till the boss said, 'Boys, just let 'em go to Hell.'

I'm goin' to the ranch to draw my money,
Goin' into town to see my Honey.

I went to the boss to draw my roll,
He figgered me out nine dollars in the hole.

So I'll sell my outfit as fast as I can,
And I won't punch cows for no damn man.

So I sold old Baldy and I hung up my saddle,
And I bid farewell to the longhorn cattle.

Jesse Chisholm

The Chisholm Trail

The Chisholm was named after a Scotch-Cherokee trader, Jesse Chisholm, who had carved out part of the path as a straight, level wagon road, with easy river fords between southcentral Kansas and his trading post on the Canadian River. It had opened as a cattle trail in 1867; in five years more than a million head had gone clumping and bawling up the road, which by then had been trampled in places to a width of 200 to 400 yards and had been cut by erosion below the level of the plains it crossed. Beside it lay the bones of cows killed in stampedes and of calves shot at birth because they could not keep up with the drives. There were the bones of humans, too, interred in shallow graves — a drowned man pulled out next to a river crossing, or an early-day trail hand or settler cut down by Indians. Every man who set out knew the risks and knew that on the trail he was considered less valuable than the cows he drove. "Look out for the cows' feet and the horses' backs and let the cowhands and the cook take care of themselves" was the trail bosses' slogan.

Sons Of The Pioneers

The Trail's Of The Cowboy

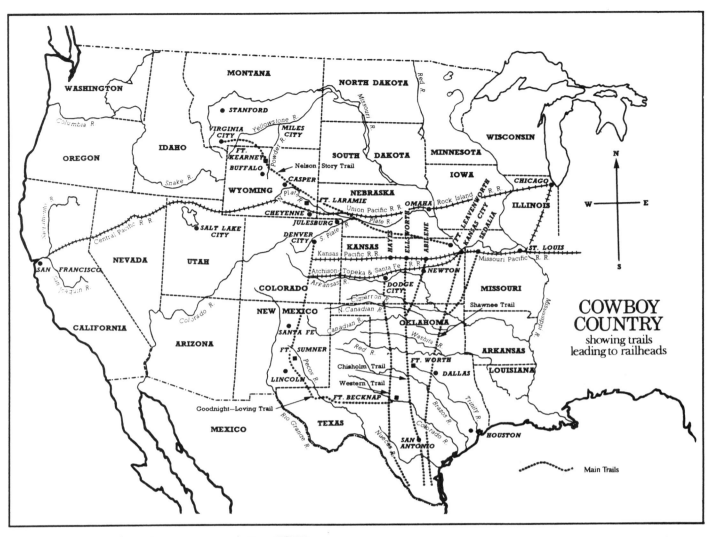

COWBOY COUNTRY
showing trails leading to railheads

·········· Main Trails

THE JIM STINSON TRAIL

(Arizona / New Mexico / Texas inset)

ARIZONA — NEW MEXICO

TONTO BASIN · SAN AGUSTIN PLAIN · Ft. Sumner · Matador
Datil · Willard · Vaughn
Socorro
Magdalena
Reserve
Ft. Apache
SALT LAKE
STAKED PLAINS LLANO ESTACADO
TEXAS

THE COLORADO TRAIL

THE NATIONAL CATTLE TRAIL

THE WESTERN TRAIL

THE WESTERN OR COLORADO TRAIL AFTER 1885

THE COLORADO TRAIL

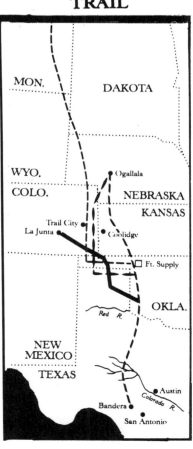

MON. — DAKOTA
WYO.
COLO.
NEBRASKA
KANSAS
Ogallala
Trail City
La Junta · Coolidge
Ft. Supply
OKLA.
Red R.
NEW MEXICO
TEXAS
Austin
Bandera · Colorado R.
San Antonio

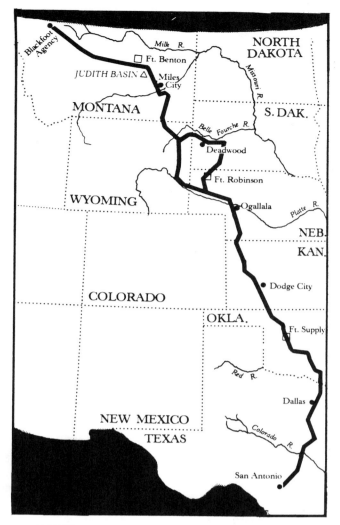

THE TEXAS-MONTANA TRAIL

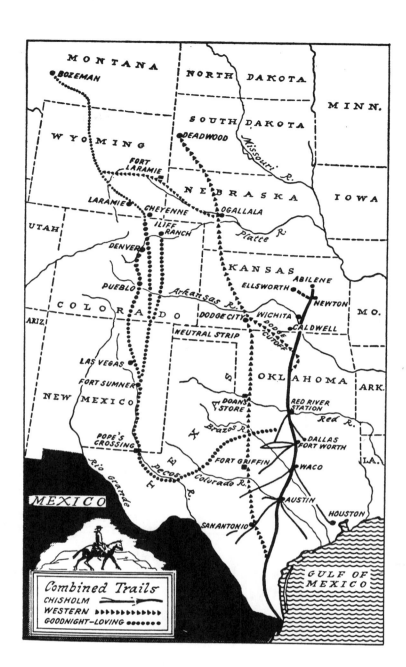

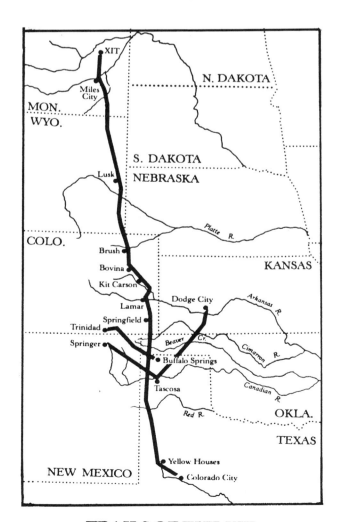

TRAILS OF THE XIT

CROOKED TRAIL TO HOLBROOK

Old Paint

One of the great night-herding songs. "Old Paint" like "Chisholm Trail", is a formula song: improvisation is easy, each singer uses his own selection of couplets. The rhythm is slow and meditative.

I'm riding Old Paint, I'm leading Old Dan,
I'm off for Cheyenne to do the hoolihan.
My foot's in the stirrup, my pony won't stand:

CHORUS:
    Good-bye, Old Paint, I'm leaving Cheyenne,
    Good-bye, Old Paint, I'm leaving Cheyenne.

Old Paint's a good pony, he paces when he can,
Good-bye, my little Annie, I'm off for Cheyenne.

Go hitch up your horses and feed 'em some hay,
And sit yourself by me as long as you'll stay.

Chorus

My horses ain't hungry, they won't eat your hay,
My wagon is loaded and rolling away.

They feed in the coulies, they water in the draw,
Their tails are all matted, their backs are all raw.

Chorus

Bill Jones had two daughters and a song,
One went to Denver, the other went wrong.

His wife she died in a barroom fight,
And still he sings from morning till night.

Chorus

Oh, when I die, take my saddle from the wall,
Put it on my pony and lead him from the stall;

Tie my bones to his back, turn our faces to the West
And we'll ride the prairie that we have loved best.

Chorus

Ernie Sites

A stern code for the XIT

In the turbulent early years of cattle ranching, cowboys had but one check on their behavior: loyalty to the rancher with whom they lived and worked. But when the big ranches came along, their absentee owners, needing to control scores of cowhands, brought in hard company rules limiting every aspect of life on the ranch. Below are only seven of the rules posted on the three-million-acre XIT spread in western Texas.

No employee of the Company, or of any contractor doing work for the Company, is permitted to carry on or about his person or in his saddle bags, any pistol, dirk, dagger, sling shot, knuckles, bowie knife or any other similar instruments for offense or defense.

Card playing and gambling of every description, whether engaged in by employees, or by persons not in the service of the Company, is strictly forbidden.

Employees are strictly forbidden the use of vinous, malt, spirituous, or intoxicating liquors, during their time of service with the Company.

Loafers, "sweaters," deadbeats, tramps, gamblers, or disreputable persons, must not be entertained at any camp, nor will employees be permitted to give, loan or sell such persons any grain, or provisions of any kind, nor shall such persons be permitted to remain on the Company's land under any pretext whatever.

Employees are not allowed to run mustang, antelope or any kind of game on the Company's horses.

No employee shall be permitted to own any cattle or stock horses on the ranch.

It is the aim of the owners of this ranch to conduct it on the principle of right and justice to everyone; and for it to be excelled by no other in the good behavior, sterling honesty and integrity, and general high character of its employees, and to this end it is necessary that the foregoing rules be adhered to, and the violation of any of them will be just charge for discharge.

Rex Allen

Poor Lonesome Cowboy

A cowboy blues with lots of self-pity. Haunted by loneliness, the absence of human companionship, far from home and loved ones, bad weather etc. A cowboy could put any amount of self pity into this night herding song; the lack of a sweetheart, a good horse, the next drink, a good meal...

I'm a poor lone-some cow - boy, I'm a poor lone - some cow-boy, I'm a poor lone - some cow- boy And a long way from home.

I ain't got no moth - er, I ain't got no moth - er, I ain't got no moth - er, To buy the clothes I wear.

I'm a poor lonesome cowboy,
I'm a poor lonesome cowboy,
I'm a poor lonesome cowboy,
And a long ways from home.

I ain't got no mother,
I ain't got no mother,
I ain't got no mother,
To buy the clothes I wear.

I ain't got no brother,
I ain't got no brother,
I ain't got no brother,
To ride the steers with me.

And I ain't got no sister,
I ain't got no sister,
I ain't got no sister,
To go and play with me.

I'm a poor lonesome cowboy,
I'm a poor lonesome cowboy,
I'm a poor lonesome cowboy,
And a long day's ride from home.

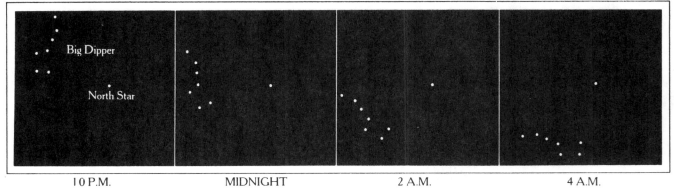

10 P.M.   MIDNIGHT   2 A.M.   4 A.M.

On clear evenings a man riding night herd could tell quite accurately when to come off shift by the position of the Big Dipper as it rotated around the North Star, making one full turn in every 24-hour period.

Liz Masterson & Sean Blackburn

The Cowboy Fiddle Band

Sons Of The Pioneers

81

What ever social life there was on the drive revolved around the chuck wagon and the camp cook in the outfit was just a little below that of the foreman or tail boss, and he used his command over the chuck to keep the hands in line, sometimes enforced with the broad end of a skillet. The root of his authority, of course, was that he provided the one element that (together with sleep) a cowboy most cherished. Here are some typical cowboy dishes, for which variations were created on the trail.

Chuck Wagon Boiled Coffee

For 4 cups of coffee, beat half an egg white with 3 tablespoons cold water and mix with 3/4 cup medium or coarsely ground coffee; put into coffee pot; add 4 cups boiling water and boil 5 minutes. Add 1/4 cup cold water and allow to stand 3 minutes to settle before serving. Crushed eggshell may be used instead of egg white, if desired.

Sonofabitch Stew

2 pounds lean beef	1 set brains
Half a calf heart	1 set marrow gut
1 1/2 pounds calf liver	Salt, pepper
1 set sweetbreads	Louisiana hot sauce

Kill off a young steer, Cut up beef, liver and heart into 1-inch cubes; slice the marrow gut into small rings. Place in a Dutch oven or deep casserole. Cover meat with water and simmer for 2 or 3 hours. Add salt, pepper and hot sauce to taste. Take sweetbreads and brains and cut in small pieces. Add to stew. Simmer another hour, never boiling.

Cowboy Beans

2 pounds pinto beans	4 tablespoons sugar
2 pounds ham hock (or salt pork)	
2 greenchilies (or to taste)	
2 onions, chopped	1 can tomato paste

Wash the beans and soak overnight. Drain, place in a Dutch oven and cover with water. Add remaining ingredients and simmer until tender. Sample the beans while cooking. Add salt to taste and water as needed.

Sourdough Biscuits

1 cup sourdough starter   1 tablespoon shortening
1 teaspoon each of salt, sugar and soda
3 to 4 cups sifted flour

Place flour in a bowl, make a well in the center and add sourdough starter. stir in salt, soda and sugar, and add shortening. Gradually mix in enough flour to make a stiff dough. Pinch off dough for one biscuit at a time; form a ball and roll it in melted shortening. Crowd the biscuits in a round 8-inch cake pan and allow to rise in a warm place for 20 to 30 minutes before baking. Bake a 425 until done.

Sourdough Starter

2 cups lukewarm potato water
2 cups flour   1 tablespoon sugar

First make potato water by cutting up 2 medium-sized potatoes into cubes, and boil in 3 cups of water until tender. Remove the potatoes and measure out two cups of remaining liquid. Mix the potato water, flour and sugar into a smooth paste. Set in a warm place until starter mixture rises to double its original size.

Red Bean Pie

1 cup cooked, mashed pinto beans
1 cup milk   1 cup sugar
1 teaspoon vanilla   1 teaspoon nutmeg
3 egg yolks, beaten

Combine ingredients and place in uncooked pie crust. Bake at 350 for 30 minutes or until set. Make meringue with the leftover egg whites; spread on pie and brown in oven.

Vinegar Pie

1 cup sugar   5 tablespoons vinegar
2 tablespoons flour   2 1/2 tablespoons butter
1 cup cold water   4 eggs, beaten

Combine sugar and flour. Add the rest of the ingredients and place in a saucepan. Cook until thick and pour into a prepared pie crust. Bake in a 375 oven until the crust is brown.

Wyoming State Archives, Museums and Historical Department

Punchin' Dough

The camp cook typically had a line of songs and stories to match anyone.
This song is for the king of the chuck

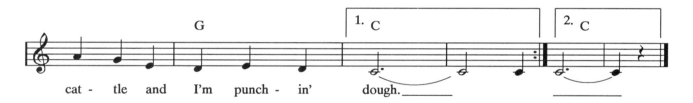

Come, all you young waddies, I'll sing you a song,
Stand back from the wagon, stay where you belong:
I've heard you observin' I'm fussy and slow.
While you're punchin' the cattle and I'm punchin' dough.

Now I reckon your stomach would grow to your back
 If it wa'n't for the cook that keeps fillin' the slack:
With the beans in the box and the pork in the tub,
I'm a-wonderin' now, who would fill you with grub?

You think you're right handy with gun and with rope,
But I've noticed you're bashful when usin' the soap:
When you're rollin' your Bull for your brown cigarette
I been rollin' the dough for them biscuits you et.

When you're cuttin' stock, then I'm cuttin' a steak:
When you're wranglin' hosses, I'm wranglin' a cake:
When you're hazin' the dogies and battin' your eyes,
I'm hazin' dried apples that aim to be pies.

You brag about shootin' up windows and lights,
But try shootin' biscuits for twelve appetites:
When you crawl from your roll and the ground it is froze,
Then who biles the coffee that thaws out your nose?

In the old days the punchers took just what they got:
It was sow-belly, beans, and the old coffee pot;
But now you come howlin' for pie and for cake,
Then you cuss at the cook for a good bellyache.

You say that I'm old, with my feet on the skids;
Well, I'm tellin' you now that you're nothin' but kids;
If you reckon your mounts are some snaky and raw,
Just try ridin' herd on a stove that won't draw.

When you look at my apron, you're readin' my brand,
Four-X, which is sign for the best in the land:
On bottle or sack it sure stands for good luck,
So line up, you waddies, and wrangle your chuck.

No use of your snortin' and fightin' your head;
If you like it with chili, just eat what I said:
For I aim to be boss of this end of the show
While you're punchin' cattle, and I'm punchin' dough.

N.EGGENHOFER

Rye Whiskey

The editor of a Dodge City newspaper estimated in 1878 that 300 barrels of whiskey were consumed in the local saloons each year. A year later an other local paper reported: "The morals of our city are rapidly improving. There are only fourteen saloons, two dance halls, and forty seven cyprians in our metropolis of 700 inhabitants".

I'll eat when I'm hun-gry, I'll drink when I'm dry,

If In-dians don't kill me, I'll live till I die.

CHORUS

Rye whis-key, rye whis-key, rye whis-key I cry.

If I don't get rye whis-key, I sure-ly will die.

1. I'll eat when I'm hungry, I'll drink when I'm dry,
   If Indians don't kill me, I'll live till I die.

   Chorus
   Rye whiskey, rye whiskey, rye whiskey I cry.
   If I don't get rye whiskey, I surely will die.

2. O whiskey you villain, you've been my downfall.
   You've beat me, you've banged me, but I love you for all.
   Chorus

3. Jack o' Diamonds, Jack o' Diamonds, I know you of old.
   You've robbed my poor pockets of silver and gold.
   Chorus

4. If the ocean was whiskey and I was a duck,
   I'd dive to the bottom and never come up.
   Chorus

5. But the ocean ain't whiskey and I ain't a duck,
   So I'll round up the cattle and then I'll get drunk.
   Chorus

6. I'll drink my own whiskey, I'll drink my own wine,
   Some ten thousand bottles I've killed in my time.
   Chorus

7. I'll drink and I'll gamble, my money's my own.
   And them that don't like it can leave me alone.
   Chorus

8. My boot's in the stirrup, my bridle's in hand,
   I'm courting fair Molly, to marry if I can.
   Chorus

9. My foot's in the stirrup, my bridle's in hand,
   I'm leaving sweet Molly, the fairest in the land.
   Chorus

10. Her parents don't like me, they say I'm too poor,
    They say I'm unworthy to enter her door.
    Chorus

11. You boast of your knowledge and brag of your sense,
    But it'll all be forgotten a hundred years hence.
    Chorus

Spanish Is The Loving Tongue

Also called "A Border Affair," Of all the cowboy love songs which sang of sweethearts true and false, this touching literary ballad has enjoyed the most sustained popularity. Its a story of true love thwarted by the barrier of "racial" differences. There is a sentiment which appeals to us all in this bittersweet ballad of the rough-hewn cowpuncher who doesn't "look much like a lover" and the senorita who whispered, "*Adios, mi corazon!*"

C. Badger Clark

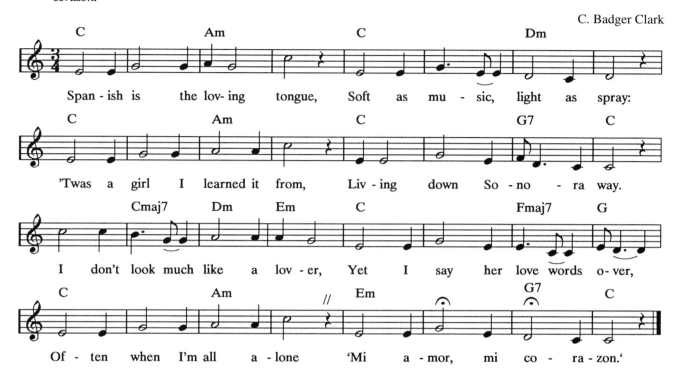

Span - ish is the lov- ing tongue, Soft as mu - sic, light as spray:

'Twas a girl I learned it from, Liv - ing down So - no - ra way.

I don't look much like a lov - er, Yet I say her love words o- ver,

Of - ten when I'm all a - lone 'Mi a - mor, mi co - ra - zon.'

Spanish is the loving tongue,	How those hours would go a-flyin'!
Soft as music, light as spray:	And too soon I'd hear her sighin'
'Twas a girl I learned it from,	In her little sorry tone -
Living down Sonora way.	
I don't look much like a lover,	*'Adios, mi corazon!'*
Yet I say her love words over,	
Often when I'm all alone -	But one time I had to fly
	For a foolish gamblin' fight,
'Mi amor, mi corazon.'	And we said a swift goodbye
	In that black unlucky night.
Nights when she knew where I'd ride	When I'd loosed her arms from clingin'
She would listen for my spurs,	With her words the hoofs kept ringin'
Fling the big door open wide,	As I galloped north alone -
Raise them laughin' eyes of hers;	
And my heart would nigh stop beating	*'Adios, mi corazon!'*
When I heard her tender greeting,	
Whispered soft for me alone -	Never seen her since that night -
	I can't cross the Line, you know.
'Mi amor, mi corazon.'	She was 'Mex' and I was white;
	Like as not it's better so.
Moonlight in the patio,	Yet I've always sort of missed her
Old Senora nodding near,	Since that last wild night I kissed her;
Me and Juana talking low	Left her heart and lost my own -
So the Madre couldn't hear;	
	'Adios, mi corazon!'

The Texas Cowboy

Many of the cowboys were floaters; they drifted from ranch to ranch, taking work where and when it was offered.   Between jobs they "rode the chuck line," enjoying the hospitality of ranchers until their welcome wore thin. With their only possessions, a horse, saddle, and "hot roll" containing bedding and a few personal things, they were on their way again. This song is one of the best of the chuck-line riders.

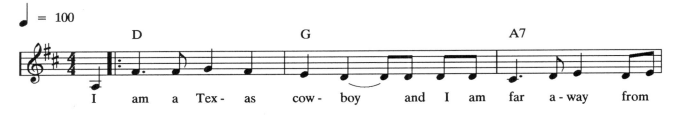

I am a Tex - as cow - boy and I am far a - way from

home. If I ev - er get back to Tex - as I____

nev - er more will roam. Mon - tan - a is too

cold for me and the win - ters are too long, Be - fore the round - ups

do be - gin my mon - ey is all gone.

Oh, I'm a Texas cowboy and far away from home,
If ever I get back to Texas I never more wll roam.

Montana is too cold for me and the winters are too long,
Before the roundups do begin, my money is all gone.

I worked out in Nebraska where the grass grows ten feet high,
And the cattle are such rustlers that they seldom ever die.

I've worked up in the sand hills and down along the Platte
Where the cowboys are good fellows and the dogies all are fat.

I've traveled lots of country, Nebraska's hills of sand,
Down through the Indian nation and up the Rio Grande;

But the badlands of Montana are the worst I ever see,
The cowboys all are tenderfeet and the dogies all are lean.

All along the Yellowstone it's cold all year round,
You'll surely get consumption from a-sleeping on the ground.

Work in Montana lasts six months in the year,
When all your bills are settled, there's nothing left for beer.

Work down in Texas lasts all the year around,
You'll never get consumption from sleeping on the ground.

Come all you Texas cowboys and a warning take from me,
And do not go to Montana to spend your money free;

But stay at home in Texas where the work lasts all year round,
And you'll never get consumption from the sleeping on the ground.

The Trail To Mexico

A night-herding song, about the heart of a woman being fickle, the cowboy's only recourse is high adventure and violent muscular activity.on the James Stinson New Mexico trail.

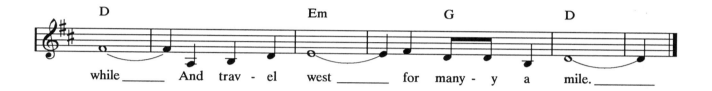

1. I made up my mind to change my way,
   To leave the crowd that was too gay,
   And leave my native home awhile
   And travel west for many a mile.

2. It was in the merry month of May
   When I started for Texas far away.
   I left my darling girl behind,
   She said her heart was only mine.

3. When I embraced her in my arms,
   I thought she had ten thousand charms.
   Her caresses soft, her kisses sweet,
   Saying, 'We'll get married next time we meet.'

4. It was in the year of '83,
   That A.J. Stinson hired me.
   He said, 'Young man, I want you to go
   And follow my herd into Mexico.'

5. Well it was early in the year
   When I volunteered to drive the steers.
   I can tell you boys, it was a lonesome go
   As the herd rolled on toward Mexico.

6. When I arrived in Mexico,
   I longed for my girl, but I could not go.
   So I wrote a letter to my dear;
   But not a word did I ever hear.

7. I started back to my once loved home.
   Inquired for the girl I called my own.
   They said she'd married a richer life;
   'Therefore, cowboy, seek another wife.'

8. 'O, curse your gold and your silver, too.
   O, curse the girls that don't prove true.
   I'll go right back to the Rio Grande
   And get me a job with a cowboy band.'

9. She said, 'Oh, buddy, stay at home;
   Don't be forever on the roam.
   There's many a girl more true than I,
   So please don't go where the bullets fly.'

10. 'Yes, I know girls more true than you,
    And I know girls who would prove true.
    But I'll go back where the bullets fly
    And follow the cow trail 'til I die.'

> **Range hands used long prods to force steers up a chute into rail cars-18 to a carload. This was a tedious chord that followed the long drive. The men hated the work, but it gave them a lasting nickname: "cowpoke."**

Windy Bill

A great boasting song. Windy Bill's flaw, though he was one of the best, was that he made his dally so he could not release the rope when old blackie, the outlaw proved too much. Being, no doubt, a bit too "windy," his prankster pals had knowingly turned him loose on a steer all had learned to respect. The moral, don't claim more than you can deliver.

Now Windy Bill was a Texas man And he could rope, you bet, He swore the steer he could-n't tie He had-n't found him yet. But the boys, they knew of an old black steer, A sort of an old out-law, That ran down in the mal-pa-is At the foot of a rock-y draw.

Now Windy Bill was a Texas man
   And he could rope, you bet,
He swore the steer he couldn't tie
   He hadn't found him yet.
But the boys, they knew of an old black steer,
   A sort of an old outlaw,
That ran down in the malpais
   At the foot of a rocky draw.

This old black steer had stood his ground
   With punchers from everywhere,
And the boys, they bet Bill ten to one
   That he couldn't quite get there.
So Bill brought out his old gray horse,
   His withers and back were raw,
And prepared to tackle that big, black brute
   That ran down in the draw.

With his Brazos bit and his Sam Stack tree
   And his chaps and taps to boot,
And his old maguey tied hard and fast
   Bill swore he'd get that brute.
Now Bill he first came a-ridin' round,
   Old Blackie began to paw,
Then flung his tail right up in the air
   And went a-drifting down the draw.

The old gray horse tore after him,
   For he'd been eatin' corn,
And Bill, he piled his old maguey
   Right around old Blackie's horn.
The old gray horse, he stopped right still,
   The cinches broke like straw,
And the old maguey and the Sam Stack tree
   Went a-drifting down the draw.

Bill, he lit in a flint rock pile,
   His face and hands were scratched.
He said he thought he could rope a snake,
   But he guessed he'd met his match.
He paid his bets like a little man
   Without a bit of jaw,
And allowed old Blackie was the boss
   Of anything in the draw.

Now here's the moral to my story, boys,
   And that you all must see:
Whenever you go to rope a snake
   Don't tie him to your tree.
But take your dally welters
   'Cordlin' to California law,
And you'll never see your old rim fire
   Go a-drifting down the draw.

Whoopee Ti-Yi-Yo, Git Along Little Dogies

This trail song was first published in 1910 by John Lomax. He first heard is sung by a Gypsy woman who was camped in a grove of trees near the cattle pens of the Fort Worth Stockyards.

1. As I was out walking one morning for pleasure,
   I spied a cowpuncher a-ridin' along.
   His hat was thrown back and his spurs were a-junglin',
   And as he approached he was singin' this song:

CHORUS

   Whoopee ti-yi-yo, git along little dogies,
   It's your misfortune and none of my own.
   Whoopee ti-yi-yo, git along little dogies,
   You know that Wyoming will be your new home.

2. Early in the springtime we round up the dogies,
   Mark 'em, and brand 'em, and bob off their tail;
   Round up the horses, load up the chuck wagon,
   Then throw the little dogies out on the long trail.
   Chorus

3. Night comes on and we hold 'em on the bed ground.
   The same little dogies that rolled on so slow.
   We roll up the herd and cut out the stray ones,
   Then roll the little dogies like never before.
   Chorus

4. Some boys go up the long trail for pleasure,
   But that's where they get it most awfully wrong.
   For you'll never know the trouble they give us
   As we go driving the dogies along.
   Chorus

5. Your mother was raised away down in Texas,
   Where the jimson weeds and sandburs grow.
   We'll fill you up on prickly pear and cholla,
   Then throw you on the trail to Idaho.
   Chorus

6. O, you'll be soup for Uncle Sam's Injuns.   It's 'Beef, heap beef!' I hear them cry.
   Git along, git along, git along little dogies; You'll all be beef steers in the sweet by-and-by. *Chorus*

The Zebra Dun

A tenderfoot on a bucking horse is the funniest sight a cowpuncher ever hopes to see. Many a song has been written around this joke. The hero of this song is luckier than most, he senses hostility from the very start, he looked like a greenhorn and talks like a dude and leads the tricksters to bait the trap which he is only too ready to spring. The boys saddled him up a bronc that "could paw the white out of the moon for a quarter of a mile." You'll have to read the song to see how he makes out.

Moderately fast

We were camped up-on the plains at the head of the Cim - ar - ron,

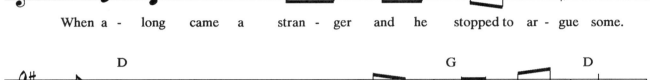

When a - long came a stran - ger and he stopped to ar - gue some.

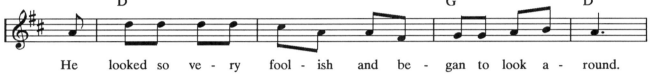

He looked so ve - ry fool - ish and be - gan to look a - round.

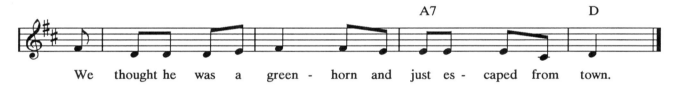

We thought he was a green - horn and just es - caped from town.

1. We were camped upon the plains at the had of the Cimarron,
   When along came a stranger and he stopped to argue some.
   He looked so very foolish and began to look around.
   We thought he was a green horn and just escaped from town.

2. We asked if he'd had breakfast and he hadn't had a sniff.
   We opened up the chuck-box and told him help himself.
   He got himself some beefsteak, a biscuit, and some beans,
   And then began to talk about the foreign kings and queens.

3. He talked about the Spanish War and fighting on the seas.
   With guns as big as beef steers and ramrods big as trees.
   He spoke about old Dewey, the fightin' son-of-a-gun,
   He said he was the bravest cuss that ever pulled a gun.

4. He said he'd lost his job upon the Santa Fe,
   And he was going across the plains to strike the 7D.
   He didn't say how come it, some trouble with the boss,
   And he said he'd like to borrow a nice fat saddle hoss.

5. This tickled all the boys to death; they laughed down in their sleeves.
   We told him he could have a horse as fresh as he would please.
   So Shorty grabbed a lasso and he roped the zebra dun,
   Then led him to the stranger and we waited for the fun.

6. The stranger hit the saddle and old Dunny quit the earth.
   He traveled straight up in the air for all that he was worth.
   A-pitching and a-squealing and a-having wall-eyed fits
   His hind feet perpendicular and his front ones in the bits.

7. We could see the tops of trees beneath him every jump.
   But the stranger he was glued there just like a camel's hump.
   He sat up there upon him and he curled his black mustache,
   Just like a summer boarder a-waiting for his hash.

8. He thumped him in the shoulders and spurred him when he whirled,
   And showed us flunky punchers he's the wolf of this old world.
   When the stranger had dismounted once again upon the ground,
   We knew he was a thoroughbred and not a gent from town.

9. The boss he was a-standing and watching all the show.
   He walked up to the stranger and he told him not to go.
   'If you can use the lasso like you rode the zebra dun,
   Then you're the man I've looked for ever since the year of One.'

10. O, he could use the lasso and he didn't do it slow.
    And when the cows stampeded he was always on the go.
    There's one thing and a shore thing I've learned since I was born:
    That ev'ry educated feller ain't a plumb greenhorn.

Bar J Wranglers

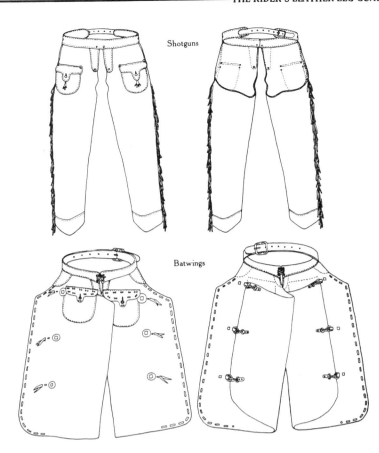

Shotguns

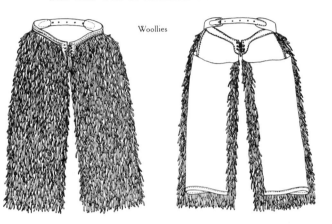

Batwings

Woollies

Before mounting up, a cowpuncher would often pull on a pair of chaps. These were seatless coverings first used by vaqueros who had to hunt cattle in heavy brush. Cowhands found they also gave good protection against rope burns, abrasions from corral poles and even horse bites.

Chaps came in three basic styles, shown here in front (*far left*) and rear views. The earlier chaps were climb-in models called shotguns, because they resembled parallel tubes. Like later chaps, they buckled at the waist. Many riders came to prefer batwing chaps, with wrap-around leggings that fastened at the back and could be snapped on without removing boots and spurs. On the cold northern ranges cowboys pulled on woollies, wintertime chaps covered on the front with wool or sometimes with fur.

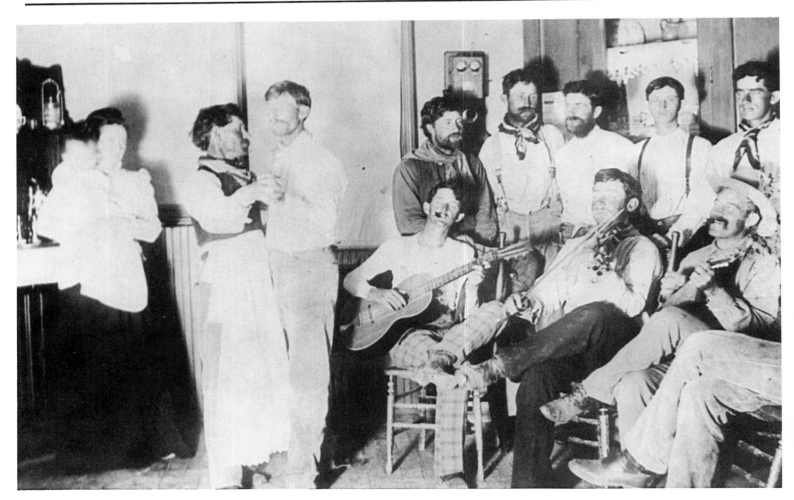

On the Lazy S in Texas two men-one heifer-branded with a frilly apron dance. The young ranch wife holding the baby for protection I suspect .

94

Songs of the Trail

Compiled by Ron Middlebrook, Foreword by Rusty Richards
Featuring songs by:
Doc Denning, Woody Paul, Chris LeDoux, Rusty Richards,
Roy Rogers Jr., Jack Hannah, Marty Robbins, Red Steagail,
Andy Parker, Ernie Sites, Michael Fleming, Frank Fara,
Peter Elman, Mason Williams, James Hobbs,
This unique book of 52 songs continues on from our popular
"Songs Of The Cowboy" book, With more of the most popular
cowboy songs from today's cowboy singers, Partial contents: Mail
Order Bride, The Last Cowboy, Gypsy Cowboy Band, Great
American Cowboy, Yellow Stud, Trail Dust, Blue Bonnet Lady,
So Long Saddle Pals, Stampede, King Of The Cowboys, Man
Walks Among Us, Pecos Bill, For Freckles Brown and many
more, plus cowboy trivia, photos, black cowboys, Spanish
cowboy ancestry, Butterfield Overland Mail Route, and much
more. 112 pages   ISBN0-931759-67-6   #00000152 $14.95

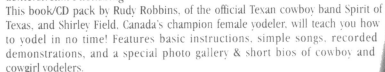